Life
Reflections

Lynda Horvath

Life Reflections

Lynda Horvath

Publication assistance and digital printing in Canada by

PUBLISHING
PageMaster.ca

Dedication

To everyone who has encouraged me on this journey, and
especially to my very patient husband, Frank!

"The best and most beautiful things in the world cannot be seen or even touched – they must be felt with the heart!"

–Hellen Keller

Peonies

I sat in my chair, and I saw leaves~~lush and green,
Just peeking over the window ledge;
A few days later, those leaves grew nice and lean,
And before I knew it, they looked like a hedge!

Soon there were tiny little buds, I could see;
Every day there seemed to be more and more;
Those little buds, they just got bigger~~oh, gee,
They looked like they would burst, right to the door!

Now, some have burst wide open, a beautiful color of pink;
They're huge, they're gorgeous, with a sweet scent;
I can see them from inside, they are my outside link;
Neighbors enjoy them~~for them, they don't cost a cent!

Cleaning Cabinets

Cleaning cabinets, a job to be done at least once a year,
Why do we have so many--five china ones in this house here!

What a lot of 'stuff' to soak, to wash, to clean, and to shine,
Guess that's why it is sometimes easier to just whine!

The figurines, the knick-knacks, the precious treasures, the dishes,
Each piece has a special meaning, many of them came with wishes!

Take everything out of the cabinet, wash the shelves, bottom and top,
Wash each precious piece, after piece, after piece--do not stop!

Don't stop till the whole cabinet has been washed, inside and out,
Then start on the next one, and the next, and the next--no time to pout.

Now just one china cabinet left, the job is almost done today,
When I'm all done--I'll have accomplished a lot--time to play!

Lynda Horvath

Face-Time

Sometimes we don't get to visit people in other cities, a few hours away,
But we are so very lucky with our social media advances of today!

Hearing a voice over a phone is always so very nice, at its best,
But seeing a face along with that voice, puts the mind at rest.

Face-Time--it really brings family and friends right into your home,
No trips down the highway, or across the country, must we roam!

We can watch our nephew's children play in their own space,
Whether it is singing a cute song, or running a three-legged race.

We can visit family members from afar, at a moment's short notice,
Don't have to clean the house or prepare a special meal--no fuss!

Friends can come into your family room any time of the day,
Good for quality time together, without even coming to stay!

Face-Time is the best--in life, such a meaningful and essential part,
Glad we can easily 'connect' with loved ones, straight from the heart!

Fall Drive

Our annual fall drive was one of the very best we have ever had,
A drive through the North Saskatchewan River Valley--not bad!

To Devon we did drive, then found two roads right down to the river,
Each led us through the trees--the beautiful scene made us quiver!

The gorgeous colors of the leaves on the trees, a sight to behold,
There were greens, browns, reds, oranges, yellows, and even gold!

The colors were stunning, like a painting right before your very eyes,
They mixed so beautifully together, like a painter's palette of dyes.

We walked amongst the crunchy fallen leaves, watched some boats,
Enjoyed the beauty on this lovely fall day--no need for our coats!

Our annual 'fall drive' is something we always look forward to do,
Next year on our drive, maybe we can include someone like you!

Lynda Horvath

I Heard the School Bell Ringing

Today the school bell rang across our busy street,
And soon the thundering of many, many running feet.

The students were out for recess, time for some good fun,
Away from books, the classroom--for fifteen minutes, done!

The loud yelling, the laughter--the happiest of childish sounds,
Having good, clean, healthy, constructive time--fun abounds!

The sound of the school bell made me a very little itsy-bitsy sad,
Thinking of the fun times I had supervising at recess--wasn't bad!

There was always a child to tell you a story of something they'd done,
Or someone to walk with you, hold your hand, feeling they'd won!

That bell--freedom for kids, not for duty-bound supervising teachers,
Nice break from classroom routines and studies--school features!

Loved that bell when I was in the classroom for those thirty-plus years,
Love it more now, hearing it from afar--shedding no 'miss-you' tears!

Down Came the Trees!

They are gorgeous to look at, their branches stretching right out,
But after many years, about fifty, they look like they're starting to pout!

They have more brownish than greenish on the inside by their trunk,
And some trees look rather sad, like they have very little spunk!

So, some people have to make a big decision—trees down, bare yard,
Or leave the ugly trees on their property and still have a privacy guard.

Our neighbors decided to get rid of two huge over-sixty-foot pine trees,
They took up too much backyard room—to the eye, not a nice 'please'!

Sad to see them go, for us it hid the back alley, and garages nearby,
The noise from the busy avenue, we now noticed—with a great sigh!

However, times they are a-changin' and we must go along with them,
'Cuz people accepted our trees gone, years ago—they were a gem!

It was fun watching the very able-bodied men take down those trees,
They certainly knew how to do it—those trees, down like a breeze!

A hard job for those folk, that was evident as we watched yesterday,
Their expertise helped our neighbor—a huge burden gone away!

Parts of an Orchestra

An orchestra has many different instruments, each its own tune,
But together they play a lovely melody, at noon or under the moon!

The guitar, as twangy as it can sometimes sound, on its very own,
Can fill in the gaps of musical wonderfulness, and set a nice tone.

The violin, as screechy as it can be, if not played just right,
Can be the softest, most beautiful sound, far into the starry night.

Take a tuba, a big instrument, with a big, deep, guttural sound,
Makes any song seem to have depth, in the orchestra pit, all around!

Our lives are like instruments, some times can be like a twangy tone,
Or like another that can be screechy, when it is played on its own.

In times of sadness and deepness, that deep, low tone we can hear,
But it is often overpowered by the sweet tones of the piano, to our ear!

I don't know much about instruments of an orchestra, not hard to see,
But I do know they all come together in one beautiful sound—one key!

And so, our lives—no matter what experiences we have been through,
Come together like a beautiful song—one that can be nicely sung, too!

Colors of the Leaves

The wonderful colors of the leaves in fall—a sight to behold!
There are so very many shades, from red and brown and gold!

There are bright green leaves, the few that are left hanging on the trees,
The ones that have not blown away, even though there's been a breeze.

The richly colored red leaves, reminding one of a poinsettia, or a red plum,
Are quickly noticed, on the tree or on the ground, like a layer of gum!

The yellow leaves, they crunch so loudly when you walk on them,
They often look just like a huge, big, bright yellowish topaz gem.

The orange leaves usually are so huge, they look like pages from a book,
One could just stare and stare at them, just can't get enough of a look!

The brown leaves—some of them have lost their pretty colors over the days,
But they still add to beauty of fall anywhere, in their own brownish ways!

The fallen leaves—they have left the trees and are now all over my lawn,
They do look so beautiful—I'll go get my leaf rake—they'll soon be gone!

Lynda Horvath

Thanksgiving Blessings

T is for the thankfulness we should show on a daily basis,

H is for our home, a place of solace, comfort and protection,

A is for all the many blessings we have, daily, in our lives,

N is for all the basic necessities of life that we take for granted,

K is for the kindness we are so fortunate to have in our friends,

S is for sharing we are able to do with those who are dear to us,

G is for giving to others regularly—our time and our talents,

I is for the immeasurable freedoms we have in this country,

V is for the valuable lessons we learn as we journey through life,

I is for interesting people who have become a part of who we are,

N is for the wonderful nation we live in, our dear Canada,

G is for gravy, cooked with the turkey and dressing—yum, yum!

It's Four-Thirty
in the Morning . . .

It's four-thirty in the morning, and what do I see?
I see my partner's eyeballs, looking right at me!

What are we doing awake at that horrible hour?
Neither of us know—can't be to have a shower!

Nothing outside has caused us to wake—no noises,
So what could be the problem—a bee that buzzes?

Can't be that, either, because it is too cold for bees,
And it wasn't my partner trying to silence a sneeze.

Was it the coffee late last night as we visited with friends?
We should be used to it by now, 'cuz our visiting never ends!

Or, maybe it was the excitement we had during the day,
As we joined friends for a walk, and in the leaves did play!

It probably is just old age, we need less sleep now that we're old,
At least that is what I have often read, or so I have been told!

I'm retired! I can sleep anytime! I can have a nap when I want,
Maybe that's my problem—no nap, go for a nice little jaunt!

Lynda Horvath

People Watching

Here I am, sitting in the lobby of a hospital, early in the morn,
Watching different people walk by, many with a bit of a scorn.

Some are not sure what the day will bring, or about their health,
A visit here may answer questions—will it improve their wealth?

Some people come in, looking lost, not sure where to go,
It's a new environment, and hospitals—what do they know?

I've seen some people talking to themselves, trying to feel calm,
And even some dear little kids, hanging tightly to their Mom.

Some people are dressed to the nine's—high heels, skirts so short,
Looks like they are off to a fashion show, maybe here at the Fort.

It's now 7:30, the cafeteria is open, the receptionist is here,
Looks like everything at this place is starting to get in full gear!

The place is humming—people coming, people going, people all around,
Quiet voices, little boy crying, lab carts going by—lots of hospital sounds!

Our Walk

We went for a walk along Lake Osoyoos, early this afternoon,
The mountain's reflections in the lake made us want to swoon!

The walk along the sandy beaches—as clear and clean as could be,
Right close to all the ducks on the lake, they're squawking at me.

Right across the lake, we could see the houses, people and roads,
It was so clear we could see everything, all except the little toads!

And then the clouds rolled in, creating a different kind of view,
The marvelous reflections were scattered, but still right on cue!

We met friendly people on our walk, often people stop to chat,
You can always find something to share about—this and that!

Around the lake we walked, looking back across—to our desert home,
What a lovely way to spend some time—we never will feel all alone!

Lynda Horvath

My Energizer Bunny

My Energizer Bunny is at it again,
It is eight o'clock on this sunny morn,
The deck furniture is all in place,
The second cup of coffee has been born.

"Why, morning is the best time of the day,"
I hear again, repeatedly over and over,
The birds are singing, the sun is shining,
And, in the green grass, there's some clover!

My energized husband, there's none like him,
With two terribly sore ankles and tired feet,
He's got a job or two to do, out of his way,
For sure, his work ethic cannot be beat!

Our yard is the first one cleaned in the spring,
The sidewalks around are clean as a whistle,
The fountain is spewing for all its worth,
And in the flowers, there is never a thistle!

Oh, I am so lucky to have a great man like him,
Who never is afraid to tackle any job at all,
He's one-of-a-kind, I'll be keeping him, for sure,
He's got a big heart, but is not really very tall!

Farming

It's late October, and driving through eastern Alberta is a treat,
Some fields have been combined, some have sheaves of wheat.

Some farmers are madly working, trying their best to be done
Their work for the season, so they can have some winter fun.

The weather has been a stickler this year—rain and snow did arrive,
At all the wrong times, many farmers certainly did not high-five!

For some, the grain was combined and laying on the ground,
Ready to be harvested, until the snow gathered all around.

The poor farmers, so dependent on the weather to survive,
They never know what their luck will bring, uplift or nose-dive!

While some of these farmers were stressed, trying to finish their work,
Others got very lucky, and farm life, for them, is just one big perk!

We often think of farmers having an easy life, compared to the city,
I applaud all those farmers, whatever their lot--they never want pity!

Lynda Horvath

Cutlery!!

'Is cutlery necessary?' I asked myself today,
Sometimes it just seems to get in my way!

Take the fork, for instance, such awkward things,
You get poked with those sharp tines, and it stings!

The table knife, often so dull it is useless to use,
It's easier to just rip things apart, less abuse!

The spoon comes in different sizes, big and small,
They're good for eating soup, but that's not all!

Really, could we just not use our fingers to eat?
It would save washing all those utensils, no treat!

One could just lick your fingers to make them clean,
It would be done in a second, no need to preen.

And the dishwasher wouldn't get jammed with stuff;
That unloading makes me sometimes huff and puff!

Enough complaints, just go with the cutlery flow,
Use them wisely--it is the best choice, you know!

Pain!!

Pain can be an ache,
Like a toothache!

Pain can be shooting,
Like the onset of a heart attack.

Pain can be burning,
Like a pinched nerve in your back.

Pain can be nagging,
Like a migraine headache.

Pain can be phantom,
Like pain when a limb is lost.

Pain can be chronic,
Like living with debilitating arthritis.

Pain can be cramping,
Like a woman with menstrual aches.

Pain can be soft tissue,
Like when you cut yourself.

Pain can be social,
Like when you lose a friend.

Pain can be emotional,
Like when you have had a bad day.

Lynda Horvath

Pain can be spiritual,
Like when you feel lost in your faith.

Pain can be intense,
Like my husband is experiencing.

Pain can BE a pain,
Not a lot one can often do!

Pain, we all experience it,
A part of life's journey!

Guests

Guests in one's home are a treat,
Whether they come to visit, or to eat!

Some come unexpectedly to your door,
They accept your home—dust and more!

Some are asked, they accept your invite,
For a chance to come for a snack-y bite!

Some come to share news with you,
Be it happy or sad, you are right on cue!

Some come to hear your new stories,
Of family experiences, you're not sorry!

Some even come with nothing in mind,
They just like to spend time with your kind!

Then there's the ones who come for a week,
You need to keep them busy, for 'quiet' you seek!

Or the ones who say they are coming and never arrive,
You make supper, and wait for them, away past five!

We have guests of all kinds and forms in our home,
We have guests come for all reasons, under our dome.

Whatever the reason, we do love all our guests, our friends,
Friendship begins in homes—friendship that never ends!

Lynda Horvath

Pasta

Some people love to eat pasta—
My husband is one such being;
It can be boiled, baked, nuked—
He loves whatever he's seeing!

There are all different kinds of pasta,
Such as lasagna, linguine, macaroni,
Rigatoni, fettuccini, and even vermicilli,
Ravioli, or spaghetti, or cannelloni.

And then there are the sauces on the top,
A simple cream or sauce of red tomato,
Spicy marinara, roasted red pepper,
Clam, or clams baked in sauce alfredo!

While all of this sounds really quite yummy
I sit here at home and drool over a menu,
Thinking what pasta I might choose to eat
At our favorite restaurant with friends and you!

Whatever it is, I'll be full so very, very soon,
'Cuz pasta usually seems to do that to me;
But the company we will be with is the best,
That's the open door to any 'supper-out' key!

Hallowe'en Candy

We bought a box of delicious candy
For Hallowe'en trick-or-treaters,
We tried to hide it, but then found it,
Guess we are just being cheaters!

The first chocolate bar tasted very good,
Let's try one more just to compare,
I like the creamy, dark chocolate one,
Frank liked them, but only by the pair!

The crispy ones, the crunchy ones, too,
They all tasted so good, so 'I-want-more',
The smooth creamy ones, and any others,
Eating Hallowe'en candy is not a chore!

So, the first box came, and then it went,
The second box came, and opened OK!
Before long, the second big box was empty,
Now, what? Hallowe'en is ten days away!

Two more boxes were bought for the kids
That might come here on Hallowe'en night,
Locks were put on the boxes of candy
So we'd have some for any trickster sight!

We made it! We still have candy to spare
For the eventful night, October thirty-one,
How we managed, I'll never ever know,
'Cuz Frank likes Hallowe'en candy, by the ton!

Lynda Horvath

I Taught Him!

I was watching TV,
And what did I see?
I saw a young man
Who I once taught.
Now, this gentleman
Holds a very responsible
And high position within
The Police Force in our city.
He is a very well-spoken man,
Very professional in his actions,
And well respected amongst
His Police Service peers.
Many years ago as a student,
He was very diligent, studious,
Well-liked by other students,
A model in the classroom,
And loved by all his teachers.
It just goes to show
That traits learned at an early age
Often continue to follow
One through-out life.
As teachers, we always said
That he would go far in life,
And we were right!
I am proud to say that
I had the utmost
Privilege to spend time
With him in an
Elementary classroom!

Why Do I Love You?

It's always good to sit back and reflect,
On someone you have as a partner, a friend,
Someone who has walked by your side
For over forty years, from beginning to end!

I love you because you are such a logical man,
Figuring out things that are above my brain,
Your fun-loving, carefree manner, most days,
Makes me just love you more, once again!

My partner, friend, husband, and mate,
Is easy to be with, any time of the day,
He thinks of others, is so considerate,
And that big smile is just a part of his way!

A great help mate, with picky inside housework,
Or work outside in the garage, or out in the yard,
He's not afraid to tackle absolutely anything at all,
No matter how easy, or no matter how hard.

That's why I love this dear man of mine,
We've grown closer and closer over time,
We've learned to give, and also to take,
And root loudly for each other, on a dime!

Yes, there are times we seem to just clash,
Our thoughts are very different and far apart,
But after all is said and done, at the day's end,
Together we are made of one beating heart!

Lynda Horvath

Learning Life Lessons

I'm watching a TV program right now,
It's about learning life lessons,
The valuable, most-useable kind!

Although they have no great ideas,
About which ones might be the best,
I'm going to find some in my own mind!

Learning to have patience is so hard,
It can make or break any situation,
And, hopefully, will keep you out of a bind!

Learning to have joy in your life-journey,
No matter the circumstances that come,
A smile on your face—should be easy to find!

Learning to have love, to give and to get,
So important to journey through life together,
Like the orange sections connected to the rind.

Learning to have peace, the gentle kind,
Sort out your challenges as best you can,
With a friend, as together you've dined!

Learning to be gracious, so hard sometimes
When life can be a bit on the rough side,
Just put all your little troubles behind!

Don't know how these life lessons stack up
To the ones they talked about on the TV,
But these are mine, the ones in my design!

Shower!

Not all showers make you wet!
Some will, like a rain shower,
Or a snow shower,
Or a sleet shower.
There could be a wedding shower,
For a bride about to be married,
Helping her set up her house,
Trying not to be harried!
There are house-warming showers,
Welcoming people to a new home,
There are graduation showers,
Celebrating goals achieved.
Every shower is a recognition
Of something being rewarded in life,
Usually lots of presents and food,
Perhaps celebrating husband and wife.
My latest shower was for a tiny baby,
A new little life was being celebrated,
She got tons of new clothes and toys,
Lots of new books to be quietly read.
What a treat it is to be part of a celebration,
A shower of any kind can be so much fun,
A lot of work to plan and organize an event,
Bet the happy hostess is glad it is done!

Lynda Horvath

Shopping Carts

Today at noon, we went out to shop,
And before long, we wanted to drop!
Drop this nonsense, going to the store,
We just come back with bags thro' our door!

Bags, bags—bags of this, bags of that,
Should have just bought a nice new hat!
A hat, I could enjoy longer than bags of food;
Which would put me in a much better mood?

I know we need groceries, that is a given fact,
But getting them requires a fair bit of tact.
Like a bull in a china shop, with a grocery cart,
Some people travel like a speeding dart.

From A to B, get out of my way—no 'please'—
My grocery cart is full, I'm in a hurry—oh, geez!
Those people are blind to anyone else in the store,
They just burst through the aisles, with a roar!

They really need traffic lights to help us folks out,
Having one-way aisles would be worthy of a shout!
Then there's the carts, in the middle of the aisle,
While their owners are looking around for a while!

Oh, goodness, this seems such a negative poem,
Today, I really should have just stayed at home.
But, we need food for company, and for us to eat,
Next time I'll go earlier—that might be a real treat!

Lunch Out!

There's a favorite place we love to go for lunch,
It is cheap, it is good, and it fills us a bunch!

First of all, the waitresses look after each table,
They are so friendly, and so caring, and so able!

It's like they are serving you right in your own home,
Sharing their life stories under the huge sky-dome!

They know what we want before we even sit down,
They have our beverages to us, quickest in our town!

The food is always very good—the ribs are so very spicy,
The loaded baked potato, the coleslaw—nothing's dicey!

We enjoy our 'ribling' meal, to the fullest of all means,
It fills our tummy's cavity, without any sticky greens!

None of us need dessert, we are all just too fed up,
Nice cold lemon water—coffee? Not even one cup!

We finish our meal, the dishes have been cleared away,
But we still have lots of visiting, so decide just to stay.

An hour or so later, we really should go back to our houses,
The waitresses continue to come by—they just 'wowz!' us!

We have a few favorite places, the ones we go to very often,
Us retired folk like to socialize and eat—both women and men!

Lynda Horvath

Cords and Passwords

We have a cord for this, and a cord for that!
What baffles me is that some are slim, some fat!

Why could they not all be the same regular-sized fit,
A one-size-fits-all would just answer the whole trick.

I guess they would lose money by having just one,
But it would sure make my life a lot more fun!

One cord for the FitBit, that's the first size,
Then another for AppleWatch gets second prize!

Then there's the MacPro computer, another one,
Then our iPads and iPhones—cords by the ton!

And then passwords—I have way more than thirty codes,
Driving me crazy, they are all different for different modes.

However, I guess we need them to keep our lives secure,
So we can live somewhat peacefully, so we can endure!

Some people have the same password for everything they do,
Not very hard to figure their lives out—quite an easy clue!

So, between cords and passwords, I can get quite irrate.
If I forget either of them, my life will soon be out-of-date.

Christmas Cards

I love Christmas cards,
The ones a friend makes,
That are so detailed and
So very personal, both to me,
And to the people who receive them!

The time and detail she 'loves'
Into these cards is amazing,
She can sit there for hours on end,
Creating and re-creating
So each one is absolutely different.

It is fun sending these special cards
To friends who you know will appreciate
And enjoy them, possibly all year long,
They are too pretty to be put away
Until next year's Christmas season!

It's sad, Christmas card-giving
Seems to be a dying event these days,
Yes, a little money on postage,
Some money to buy a card,
But, are friends not worth it?

I love getting a card, but more than that
I love sending a card—not an email
Or a text message, but a real card,
Sent with real love and care, and
Real "Merry Christmas" wishes!

Lynda Horvath

Mountains

The mountains just outside our Osoyoos window,
Are stunning, so picturesque, just all-in-a-row!

Some tops are peaked, some are rather curvy,
To get to the top of any of them would be nervy!

Some have nice green trees all the way to the top,
Some of them—half-way up the mountain, they stop!

The mountain right in front of me looks like an old face,
With wrinkles and more wrinkles, each has its own place.

The gullies and crevices, the valleys, the gorges so deep,
They all make up the mountain's great features, all in a heap!

The clouds often hang low, sometimes over the mountaintops,
Or settled into the many valleys, making picture-perfect stops!

The mountains have been standing, erect for very many years,
They've sheltered lakes and towns, even created many fears.

Lurking mountains can be ominous, seeming to lord over the land,
To me, they are very protective, rising before us, close at hand!

I love to watch these mountains, their image reflected in the lake,
This scenery I can watch forever, every little moment I am awake.

It's Easy to Get Ready

For some people, Christmas is a time of stress,
A time of frustration, tough relationships, and duress.

Buying gifts, spending money one does not really have,
Don't have family to be with, or too much family—which half?

And so, by the time Christmas Day comes on the twenty-fifth,
Some may wish it was over, others are glad to get a nice gift!

Our Christmas is easy—our family is very small, and not that pressed,
To spend money on needless gifts, or to get overly stressed.

Spending time together is what most of us seem to value more,
Getting together, having a visit, sharing time, within someone's door.

Although we don't all agree, those we spend time with at Christmas,
Are the ones who take us as we are, want to be together with us.

One cannot put a monetary value on minutes and hours shared,
With your family and friends, with those who really have cared!

Our Christmas get-togethers have been stretched over many days,
So we can share time with many friends and family—all A-OK!

So, getting together is easy, and the greatest gift to receive,
Forget the presents, the stress—enjoy friendships that never leave!

Lynda Horvath

The Beginning of a New Year

It's exciting—it's the beginning of a new year,
We have no idea what is before us, that is clear!

We will have some sadness, there is no doubt,
But we'll have many blessings—so we can shout!

Each day will be different, we are prepared for that,
Will it be to visit, to clean the house, or just to chat?

Each day spent with family, with friends—we have lots,
Both near and far, we continue to connect with their dots.

This year started, being away from our Edmonton home,
But with our dear son and his sweetie—we were not alone.

If the rest of this year is anything like this first 2018 day,
We will be very happy this year, in many-a special way!

So, twenty-eighteen, bring it all on, we are ready for you!
We'll make every day a blessing—let's see what we can do!

Up the Mountain

We decided to take a trip
Up the mountain to the east
Of our winter town.

The weather in our town
Was warm, lovely, springy
And a 'breath of spring'.

As we went up the highway
Toward the mountain top,
We were met with snow!

Not a little bit of snow,
But about a foot of it,
Covering the ground.

We toured down a few roads,
Rutty, slushy, some snow-plowed,
But very wintry, indeed!

Some sub-divisions had homes
Already built, some very large,
Many just deserted homes.

 Lots of driveways were not used,
Obviously no one is there,
Enjoying this winter wonderland.

Lynda Horvath

The view from many of the lots
Is absolutely gorgeous, just stunning,
Catching one's breath with the beauty.

People, we are told, have walked away
From many of these beautiful homes,
Leaving them to just rot and decay.

Such a lovely drive, so much to see,
Sunshine and clouds in every direction,
Absolutely mouth-dropping scenes.

Fog!

Fog slips in between the mountains
Like a quiet thief at night;
It settles in, high or low,
Not caring about the height.

Wherever it decides to stay,
The clouds are so fluffy white,
In amongst the mountains and hills,
Creating quite a lovely sight.

A little boy out on this lovely day,
Underneath that fog, will lose his kite;
An adult driving a car down the road
Will need to stay to the right.

A senior, going out for a walk
Will hold onto his cane, real tight;
The fog seems to create a cover,
One that lets in not much light.

But rather it smothers and covers
Any ground area—a blurry site;
The fog is beautiful, no matter what,
Even though it takes a big bite . . .

Lynda Horvath

Out of the earth's visible beauty,
Maybe scary even to a little sprite;
There is nothing we can do about the fog,
Try as we think we might.

So we just must learn to enjoy it,
As one of earth's beauties so bright,
I love how it slinks in and slinks out,
Across the lake, day or night!

It's a Smaller World

The other day we met some folk as we ate our lunch,
Before we knew it, we had mutual friends—a bunch.

So, we decided to meet for coffee—that happened today,
We soon discovered other connections along our life's way.

As we sat and visited, another couple came into the shop,
We had met them a week or two ago, at a music hip-hop!

The more we all shared, the more hilarious it all became,
Soon we realized we knew more than one common name.

This one knew this person who was friends of yet another
Who lived in the same place or town as another's brother.

Then, it became even more obvious that this world had shrunk,
When two people realized they had bought each other's junk!

Lots of laughter shared, lots of common experiences, too,
We decided we would meet again soon—follow our life's cue.

So, until next time, we might figure out some more similar events,
That will bring more laughter—something might even make sense.

Lynda Horvath

The Ducks and Geese

We get into bed at night,
Open the patio door,
Snuggle down under the covers,
Silence–no more!

Our building is very quiet,
No one seems to be about,
No noise, no footsteps,
No one giving a shout!

It's not the noise in the building,
It's not the cars from the street,
It's not my partner snoring (yet),
It's not our phones going 'tweet'.

This noise is, however, extremely close,
Right from the lake outside our door,
The ducks and geese, there are many,
At least a hundred or maybe even more!

Those birds, so noisy with all their quacking,
They start to flap around, and then to squawk,
For hours on end, they never seem to stop,
They are worse than people who like to talk!

However, I must not complain, it really isn't that bad,
It is actually quite comforting to know, just outside
Our patio windows are excited and happy little birds,
Who like to chat together, swim together and glide!

Groundhog Day

February second, every year, is important,
It is the day of the year for the groundhog,
The day the groundhog makes decisions
For all the weather-people that are watching.

These weather-people depend on the groundhog
To let them know if spring is near or far away,
It is either around the first 'spring-ish' corner,
Or another six weeks of winter is on its way.

There are a number of groundhogs around the country
Who all will pop out of their holes to see the world
On this chosen day in early February, the second,
To see if the sun is shining brightly, or not at all.

This year, a couple of the groundhogs saw their shadows,
So we will have another six weeks of winter weather,
Another couple of groundhogs did not see their shadow at all,
That means spring will come early this year—yeah!

Well, even the groundhogs are confused this year,
So, I guess we will just have to wait and see what happens
With our weather—whatever comes, winter or spring,
We will enjoy each and every day, regardless of Mr. Groundhog!

Lynda Horvath

Wine and Cheese Pairing

Up to a winery for a little tour
Of the amazing finery there,
We started with the gift shop
Before we went to wine/cheese pair!

So many delicious dips and jellies
One can try, and purchase there,
Good on crackers of all kinds,
Always good enough to share.

Tasting five different wines, we did,
First, just out of the bottle, so pure,
Then an appealing appetizer we had
Before we tried the wine again, for sure!

We couldn't get over the taste difference
Before and after our appetizer treat,
A totally different palate experience we had,
Some new and different wines we did meet.

One appetizer was part of a grilled cheese sandwich
With apple slices thinly sliced in the sandwich middle,
Another was a dried apricot, with a pecan over that,
Then blue cheese on top, as strong as a fiddle.

The other appetizers were just as interesting,
And did their job with the wine/cheese pairing,
A delightful afternoon at the local winery,
Glad we all were just a little bit wine-daring!

Every River Needs a Bridge

At a music jam recently, we heard
That 'every river needs a bridge',
And it stuck with both of us.

So, we had a large discussion
About why a bridge might be needed
Across a river, any river.

Rivers can be narrow, or they can be wide,
They can have rushing waters,
Or be very calmly flowing.

Rivers can be too deep to wade across,
Or they can be too rocky to walk across,
Or even too fast-moving to go near.

Lynda Horvath

What is on the other side?
Do we really need to know what is there?
Will it make our life any different?

The only way we will ever know what awaits us,
Is to cross that beam, or truss, or arch bridge,
Or a cantilever, or a cable bridge.

Regardless, it will take us to the other side
Of a river, or valley, or canyon, or gorge,
The very easiest way possible.

Oh, the bridges of life take us across
Many rivers of experiences so we always can
Look back to see the beautiful 'other side'.

My Boy!

Today is Valentine's Day!
But, more importantly,
It is my dearest son's birthday!
A day in the calendar year
That is very important to me!
A day I will never forget,
Forty-eight short years ago,
But remembered every year since
That very special day!
Quite a bundle I did bring home
That next week, a hungry bundle,
Who could not get filled up.
Against the advice of everyone,
The only way I could satisfy
That hungry little ten-pounder
Was to feed him pablum

Lynda Horvath

(Very much against the 'rules')
The day I brought him home.
Pablum and fruit, of any kind,
Were his favorites from day one.
Red hair, about an inch all over
His precious little head,
A show-stopper in the baby nursery
By everyone who saw him.
Cute little cheeks, a little round nose,
The sweetest baby on that ward.
Now, my little man has grown up
To be a fine gentleman,
A professional in his career,
Full of compassion, and caring,
Someone whom I am very proud of,
A young man I am so very pleased
To call my darling, loving son!

Cooking!

What, oh what, shall I cook today?
It is getting very boring, I must say.

Trying to figure out something new,
Is like trying to tie an old velcro shoe!

It is easy to have the 'same-old' menu,
One gets tired of the lack of something new.

So, let's think about dessert for this meal,
Cinnamon buns, pie—what will appeal?

Then there's the salad—crispy, green kale?
Maybe not the greatest—but it was on sale!

Any veggies? Corn or peas—so tired of those,
Some carrots, or spinach—a double dose!

The potatoes—what will we do—mash, or bake,
Or make them into a nice fried, crispy potato cake?

Now we've got this yummy meal almost figured out,
Check the freezer for meat—quite necessary, no doubt!

Cooking, so hum-drum each and every day, for two,
I'd rather cook for twenty—it is so much easier to do!

Lynda Horvath

What Can I be Thankful for Today?

A—a bright and interesting future ahead
B—blessings, not one by one, but ton by ton
C—children, mine, who bring me great joy
D—delightful, exciting privileges in life
E—experiences you have had to make you grow
F—freedoms, the many I have in this land
G—gratitude for the help people have provided
H—hugs, a hug a day keeps the doctor away
I—interesting people you meet in life
J—justice for all, regardless of differences
K—kindness to one another, daily
L—love, so easy to give to those who accept it
M—marriage, one I am very content with
N—new challenges, may I be always ready
O—opportunities that have made me who I am
P—people who have come into my life for a reason
Q—quiet times of reflecting my life's journey
R—relatives that I love to be around
S—special visitors to our home
T—teaching, my wonderfully chosen career
U—unique trials that make us grow
V—valuable lessons in seventy plus years
W—winter, our Osoyoos home and family
X—x-tra special times with old friends
Y—yams, my favourite vegetable
Z—zero tolerance, be respected and respectful

No More Cinnamon Buns?

No more cinnamon buns?
I have made twenty-nine batches,
That have disappeared, quickly,
Down many people's hatches!

Cinnamon buns for laundry days,
Between the wash cycle and the dry,
Cinnamon buns for many coffee parties,
And often to wish someone 'good-bye!'

Some were made for special birthday parties,
Some for visitors who came for a meal,
Others for some new friends 'just-because',
And others to seal up a friendly deal!

Lynda Horvath

Cinnamon buns—not sure why they were a hit,
But the more I made, the more I had to make,
To keep all our friends' tummies pleasantly full,
So, the bread-maker would again come awake!

The most buns anyone ate at once was eight,
The next managed to get six under his belt,
What a joy it is to see someone enjoy these buns,
For me, making these treats it is truly heartfelt!

Cinnamon buns, cinnamon buns, I'll make more,
Everyone seems to enjoy them, such a treat,
They are easy to do, just need three hours,
And I'll have made something tasty to eat!

Home!

Home is where your heart is,
With all your familiar surroundings,
Knowing what is in every corner,
In every cupboard and on each shelf.

All one's various pictures on the walls
Have special meanings and memories,
They've been hanging there for years,
They make our house a home!

It is nice to sleep in your own little bed,
It is cozy, it is soft, it is warm, it is inviting,
And, your kitchen, filled with all you need,
To cook, to bake, to roast, to serve company.

Lynda Horvath

Home can be a lot of work to keep up,
To keep it neat and tidy and welcoming,
It sometimes causes one to be gloomy,
With all (you think) that must be done!

But when you are away from your home
For a lengthy period of time, three months,
You miss all those special things that make
Your daily life so much easier, and fun!

So, home—where one puts a lot of years
Into making a house reflect your tastes,
And contains many memories of your life,
There is no place better—your own home!

What is a Hero?

What is a hero? Let's check it out,
In the dictionary—give it a shout!

A hero, known for courageous acts,
Or nobility of character, them's the facts.

Or, a person whose abilities are so great,
Achievements are part of their mandate.

A hero can be a mentor of yours, or an idol,
Whose life has been very complete and full.

Usually a hero is someone you can look up to,
Someone whose values are tried and true.

So who is my hero? I do have a few of them,
Each have added to my life, each--a real gem.

Lynda Horvath

My Grade Three and Grade Six teachers, gems for sure,
Impacted my life in ways that I now realize were pure.

They taught me lots, especially in ways I didn't realize,
They quietly taught me to believe in myself, to rise!

To rise above the trials, the hardest parts of my journey,
To make each day count, to be the best that I could be.

There are others who influenced me, they are heroes, too,
Thanks for their positive input, they gave me many-a clue!

In different ways, each helped me, taught me, guided me,
Let me thank them today by living my life to a 'hero's T!"

Yappy Dogs

We HAD a quiet neighborhood
Until some yappy dogs did arrive,
Some are just a few doors away,
Some another direction do thrive!

The ones across the lane are loud,
They bark at anything in the lane,
Whether it is a car or someone walking,
They show their yappiness—a pain!

The ones a few doors down, used to be one,
Then another arrived, and they compete,
Who will be the loudest, the most noticed,
On our used-to-be quiet little street?

And then the four of them, across the fences,
Snarl and bark at each other when they're out,
They are so very annoying to us, to everyone
Who lives within the block, or there about!

Lynda Horvath

The owners seem to think this barking is OK,
Early in the morning, late at night, whenever,
They just seem to put the dogs outside to visit,
Whatever and whenever with whoever—Grrrr!

There must be something we can do to stop this,
To retrieve our quiet neighborhood once again,
Our neighbor gets the noise more than we do,
And maybe has a solution to stop this pain!

I know people love their pets, I do not disclaim,
But keep them quiet, think of others around,
Who could enjoy them as well, as they walk by,
And peace on this block could again abound.

Easter

Easter is coming,
It is early this year,
It is happening in March,
And that is right here!

According to the old calendars,
Easter can come most any time,
From late in March till late in April,
Which makes no reason or rhyme.

As long as it comes, that is the fact,
So we all can have a holiday or two,
To celebrate the way we should,
And have a good Easter feast, too!

Lynda Horvath

Sometimes Easter is filled with family,
Sometimes it is filled with your friends,
Whatever the case, let's do our best
To make sure this spring event never ends.

Let's cook to our hearts content,
Let's have fun with whoever is here,
Let's enjoy each other's company,
And hold each other very dear!

For it doesn't matter who you see
At this time of the year,
Just rejoice for the meaning of it,
And spread lots of great cheer!

It's Spring Break

It is Spring Break here this week,
There are many happy kids around,
The teachers, too, taking a peek,
No entry or recess bells abound!

Many people take this time to go
Away on a holiday somewhere,
Get away from our weather, our snow,
For a few rays of sun, over-there!

Away from the tests, and the books,
Away from early mornings, and alarm,
Now to sleeping in, time to be cooks,
Now to forgetting calendars—no harm!

So, whether you stay home or away you go,
Life this week is meant to be different—yes!
It is to be a week of relaxing, just being slow,
Whatever you do, even if you create a mess!

I used to love, years ago, my Spring Break week,
Even if it meant just being at home, be a laze,
I love Spring Break this year even better—eek!
Just another week in retirement's great daze!

Lynda Horvath

April Fool's Day

Today is April Fool's Day, a day set aside for fun,
For some people, it is a day when trickery is done!

For my friend from school days, it is her birthday,
It is for our uncle, as well--his very special day!

People play tricks on each other, some not very funny,
Like pretending one's pregnant--really not nice, Honey!

One time when I was a kid on the farm, many years ago,
Some neighbors took our milking machines, and did stow!

They stowed them a half-mile away, in our rural mailbox,
And my parents were seething, right through their socks.

It took us a while to find them, the cows waiting in the barn,
It really wasn't very funny, but they really didn't do any harm.

It was just very inconvenient, very hard for Mom all alone,
To get on with her milking chores, on our rural farm home.

It was supposed to be an April Fool's joke, but it was too much,
Very costly farm property could have been broken, and such.

So April Fool's is not one of the days in which I usually take part,
If we have to have fun, just do something silly, but from the heart!

One Day at a Time

One day at a time, that is life's story,
We need to live each day, with no regrets,
Life with differences will never be much fun,
Put them aside, if possible, before the sun sets.

Isn't it great that we live each day on its own,
Those twenty-four hours—we do as we please,
Trying to be a good citizen, follow the rules,
Having fun with friends, taking time for a tease!

If we knew exactly what tomorrow would bring,
Would we really live our life very much different,
Would we still make mistakes, maybe even more,
And maybe even regret a day that was ill-spent?

Lynda Horvath

I know what I have tentatively planned for tomorrow,
I know I have a few jobs that should be done,
But between now and then, who really knows,
It might end up just a day of pure, clean fun!

Almost seven years ago, the phone call, unexpected,
To say my Dad had left this world, his life over,
That really brought home that we never do know . . .
So make the most, as if you have a four-leaf clover!

May I make the best of each day, be helpful and kind,
Treat others with the greatest of respect and love,
Realize and recognize differences and attitudes,
I know that I'll need lots of great help from above!

Purging Stuff

I'm taking an empty box,
Going from room to room,
Finding 'stuff' I no longer need,
Or no longer use—kaboom!

Into the box that stuff will go,
And out to a friend's garage sale,
If I haven't used it, or worn it,
In a whole year—it is time to bail!

The cupboards and shelves, so full,
Of all that stuff we had to buy,
Used once or twice, maybe a bit more,
Now it sits, on a shelf up high!

So, the time has come, I am serious,
Before we decide to move, let's declutter,
So when we have to make a move,
We will have no need to mutter.

Lynda Horvath

One box out of each room, that is my goal,
Some maybe will have even two or three,
But, whatever, it is going to be done,
This week—I'm going to be a busy bee!

Someone else may get some use of my stuff,
Someone else may use it with great joy,
But the greatest joy will be having cleaned up,
And feeling good—that, I will really enjoy!

Class Reunion

It's been fifty-five long years since Grade Twelve grad,
We've all had some great life-times, and some even sad.

We've all grown older, a few wrinkles are now well seen,
Our hair has grown greyer, or whiter, or none on our bean!

Some of us have a few shades of our memory gone south,
And we can't always be sure what will come out of our mouth!

Regardless of all this, we managed once again to meet,
It is always fun to see whom we can, by their name, greet!

Forty of us, once again, spent a few hours together to chat,
We covered every topic and school experience, just like that!

It was such a great time, we decided to do it again very soon,
While we all have our faculties, and before they live on the moon!

Lynda Horvath

Rained-Out Barbeque

A bunch of us classmates were getting together once again,
At a friend's country home, just when it started to rain!

Now rain cannot dampen spirits, when laughter does abound,
It just makes the occasion livelier, 'cuz we're all fun-bound!

We all brought a bit of the delicious supper, just to help out,
Such a variety was before us, one could not help but shout!

Shout for joy, for a number of reasons that were right at hand,
We all love being together, and all lived in that part of the land.

We all love to help each other, when we get together like this,
And will do anything we can to be present, and not to ever miss!

Our rained-out barbeque gave us lots of time to visit and to chat,
Anywhere—together--you just cannot beat a great day like that!

Warm Weather

We must be getting old, we cannot stand this warm weather,
Our dear, old bodies are feeling like a soggy piece of leather!

We are surrounded by fans, in every room of this house,
We wish we had a hole in the ground like a little old mouse!

No matter what we do, we are sweating and feeling worn right out,
This thirty-degree weather is just making us both seem to pout!

And the lawn, and the flowers, we just can't seem to water enough,
They are so dry and crinkled—for them it, too, is really quite tough!

A day like today, we think of the coolness of a snowflake or two,
But then quickly realize, we would have to be wearing a big shoe!

No sandals to be worn in the winter, I must quit complaining right now,
Rejoice in the warm weather—it really is quite beautiful—wow!

Lynda Horvath

Half Over

The year is half over—oh, my, where did those six months go?
Seems just like yesterday we were celebrating New Year's
With our kids from the west coast, amidst the deep snow,
Enjoying every minute—no fears, and certainly no tears!

Our winter-away time was an experience, for three months
We were busy, met great people, attended super events,
Had a lot of fun, and made some dear, life-long friends,
From New Brunswick to Saskatchewan, ladies and gents.

Some of our time was a bit of a stretch, but we learned a lot,
About relationships, about being too helpful, about our life,
About who we really are in the eyes of others--family and friends,
But we have decided to look on the positive, not on the strife!

Our time since then has been busy, uplifting and fun with dear friends,
We have achieved a number of bucket-list goals, have gone places
We had never been, and enjoyed every minute—off to Vancouver,
Great times—always a 'treat' to spend time with new faces!

The Tree Stump

A huge tree grows over the years,
It weathers the storms and rain,
It survives the winters of snow,
Its leaves drop, then grow again!

Over the years, it just becomes bigger,
From a mere stalk of a little seedling,
To branches spreading to the sun,
Becoming like a huge, moving swing.

Then, eventually, that tree must come down,
When it gets just too big, or maybe it dies,
It leaves a huge hole in the landscape scene,
Merely because of this beautiful tree's size!

So what is left to be seen of this gorgeous tree?
Now, there is merely a stump left in its place,
A stump showing where a sturdy tree once stood,
A stump, that over the years, was a solid base.

The stump can become a place on which to sit,
Or it can become a base for a nice plant in a pot,
It could be a table for a summer garden tea party,
It could be useful, lots of ideas can be caught!

Or, the tree stump can be ground down
Right to its thick, deep, roots underground;
If this happens, soon the stump will disappear
And the tree that was there—no longer around!

Lynda Horvath

Bird Feeder

We bought a bird feeder a year or so ago,
It went unnoticed by our bird-friends, it seems;
So we bought another bird feeder yesterday,
And some different food, too—Bird Dreams!

Well, within an hour, a flock of birds did arrive,
They chomped and they chewed like crazy;
They ate, flew away, came back, ate some more,
One thing is certain—they surely are not lazy!

Before the day was over, the small feeder was empty,
Every kernel of seed was gone, (some on the ground),
The birds just kept coming for a visit to the feeders,
As we sat there watching them, not making a sound.

They were most entertaining, those tiny little folk,
As they hustled around the feeders with such ease,
It seemed they were so happy with some new food,
Could almost hear them say 'Thank You!' after 'Please!'

Well, they are our newest entertainment, these birds,
We should have bought new feeders and new food
Long ago—oh, well, better late than never, they say,
'Cuz we're enjoying the new bird feeder—real good!

Fly-Tying

I am trying something new to do,
Not sure if I have enough smarts,
I will give it a good-hearted try,
With all those tiny little parts!

Haven't a clue what a fish likes,
What might get it to bite a hook,
Is it the feather, or the sparkle,
Maybe I should check my new book!

Start with the vice, get the hook set,
Thread the bobbin, wind it around,
Make a nice base, then start to build
Your 'fly' creation—it 'may' be found!

Choose the feather—for wings, or tail,
Then the color—red, blue or green,
Around a black, thick chenille body,
Maybe a sparkler, to better be seen.

Lynda Horvath

Just winding and tying the thread,
Important to do just tight, and right,
To secure the wings, and the tail,
And, to entice the fish to bite!

It is a very delicate task to try to do,
With the thread, colors, add-on's, too,
But each time you finish one tied-fly,
You seem to have just one more clue.

A lesson from an experienced fly-guy,
Showed me that I was on the right track,
If I just keep busy trying to improve,
Hopefully, I will get the proper knack!

Sheep

Once I had a little lamb for a pet,
Mary was her name—oh, so sweet;
She was fed from a baby bottle,
And followed me, right at my feet!

Now, she was a relative of a goat,
Only much, much more stocky;
Although she was quite a timid sort,
She often tried to be a bit cocky!

A cud-chewing mammal, she was,
On nice green grass she loved to graze,
Although she was just one little lamb,
Within a flock, was her best maze.

As sweet as a little baby lamb can be,
Its instincts and its own ways to protect
Itself are really not all that great, it seems,
As predators often make them wrecked.

Lynda Horvath

A baby sheep, called a little lamb,
Is raised by its mother, known as ewe,
Its father, a ram, completes the family,
All usually found on a farm, it's so true!

Sheep can be raised for milk or meat,
But most of all for their thick, fluffy wool,
The sweetest of animals, gentle and regal,
Mary, my little sheep, made my life full.

Wolves

We all can learn a lesson from a wolf pack
And how they travel together, in a space.

The three in front are often old and sick,
Always walking at the front, to set the pace.

The next five are the strongest of the wolves,
Protecting the front three from any attack.

The middle group now is fully protected,
Travelling along, they have nothing to lack.

The five behind the larger middle group,
Are also among the strongest of the team.

These five have an important job, as well,
To protect the back of the middle, it'd seem.

The last wolf is the leader of this pack,
He ensures no one is ever left behind.

He keeps the pack tight, on the same path,
Ready to run any direction to protect his kind.

So what can we learn from the life of a wolf,
One that is very protective, one can deem.

Being a leader is not about being in front,
It is about taking care of your entire team.

Lynda Horvath

My Dad's Chair

One time, many years ago, my Dad
Was working in an office at their home,
And did not have a very decent chair
To sit, to do his paperwork, like a gnome.

So out he went to a garage sale or two,
And found a sturdy old wooden chair,
That seemed to be just what he needed
To plan his working days—from here to there!

That sturdy old chair served him well for years,
It was his 'throne' to finish all his daily work;
And when his days of working were over,
And he moved, that chair became my 'perk'!

I love that chair, it is comfy and well built,
The firm seat, straight back—just so great,
For when I need to just quietly sit and relax,
It really has become my 'solitude mate'.

I'm so glad I have it to enjoy each day,
Glad it will always be a part of our home,
For without it today, I would not be sitting
On it, and writing this short 'chair' poem!

House Plants

House plants can be very nice,
When they are healthy and green,
When they flower and even bloom,
The best you have ever, ever seen!

But then one week you forget the water
That helps keep them nourished and fed,
And before you know it, along comes a leaf
That looks less healthy, and more dead.

They need plant food, once in a while,
But when did I last give them some?
It may have been within the last month
Or maybe it was three months? Ho-hum!

So, I have sort of decided this morning,
Looking at my plants in various stages,
That maybe phony ones would be better,
But, really, that would be outrageous!

I guess I will try to revive some of them,
They do deserve my attention and care,
And some other day I'll make up my mind,
To get rid of them, or leave them right there!

Lynda Horvath

Favorite Spot

We had lunch today at a very favorite spot,
We love their meals, and the waitress, too;
We met with some very great friends,
A birthday to celebrate, not something new!

The riblings, the baked potato, and coleslaw,
Are always so tasty and tender and great,
Before we knew it, we all looked down
At a completely food-less, empty, plate!

These two folk we love to meet with often,
Are always so positive and friendly and fun,
There are lots of laughs, lots of deep talk,
And our conversation topics—never are done!

It is friends like them, whom we love to be with,
A pleasant, relaxing, and joyful time together;
We can say what we want, without a worry,
And not have to even think about the weather!

One of our very favorite spots to enjoy a meal,
Two of our very favorite people we do know;
Put those fav's together, and what do we get,
Why, a wonderful time without going to a show!

Mother's Day

Don't know why they have Mother's Day,
'Cuz, really, every day is a day for a mother!

Once you become a mother, the task is set,
Twenty-four hours a day, you are no other!

From the time of their birth, your life is busy,
With caring for a little, tiny life so sweet.

Soon they are walking, busier you are now,
And to hear them talking is quite a treat.

Before you know it, they are off to school,
Graduation and college become the norm.

Soon they've found a career of their choice,
And a partner to share their home-dorm!

All this time, you have fretted and stewed,
About choices your child made in their life.

You haven't stopped 'mothering' yet at all,
You worry about each pleasure and strife.

You want only the best for them every step,
'Cuz that's what you do in a mothering way!

Being a mother is a full time job, no doubt,
But we all agree this job is really quite okay!

Lynda Horvath

Spring Plants

Today was the day, off to the store
To get a dozen plants, maybe more!

Ready are the barrels, baskets and pots,
Ready for pretty flowers, lots and lots!

What kinds shall we get now this spring?
The same as last year, or ones that sing?

The choice is usually very great and vast,
This year, not so much as it was in the past!

However, dracaena and alyssum, salvia, too,
Petunias, verbena, and hanging ones—two!

Dusty miller, lavender, marigolds, ageratum,
When these are all planted—I'll be done!

The pots look so nice, winter has all gone away,
And these pretty flowers—spring is here to stay!

Now, to keep them fed and watered, in the sun,
Means this chore will turn out to be great fun!

Sitting on the deck, on some hot summer days,
I'll be glad I planted flowers under the sun's rays!

Where is Fall?

Here it is, September 12th!!!
A wonderful fall day, but
Some white stuff has covered
Our entire yard!!!!
This 'stuff' is called snow,
And has arrived very early this fall!
In fact, one week earlier
Than it did last year!
Thankfully, it all melted
Within a few days!
Then—surprise, surprise—
Just three days later,
It snowed again!
Big, white snowflakes fell all over
Our wonderful city!
Then, it all melted,
Once again!
Lo, and behold,
The third time this month,
Just the next week,
We had another huge dump!
WHAT is happening
To our weather this year?
Cities south of here
Have had more snow than us,
And are barely digging out
From underneath this SNOW!
So, with these bouts of snow,
I wonder where our fall did go!

Lynda Horvath

Happy Birthday, Canada!

It's Canada's birthday today,
The first day of July every year!
I have so much to be thankful for,
Mostly because I live right here!

Living right here in Canada,
Edmonton, Alberta, to be exact,
It has been my home for decades,
Fifty-six years, as a matter of fact!

I love my country, a beautiful place,
The gorgeous mountains, the flat prairies,
Rushing rivers, the rolling country-side,
All make up a land where I'm happy to be.

This country has been good to me,
It has kept me safe over the years,
I have had lots of laughter here,
And sometimes even a few tears!

But the laughter and tears aren't what make
This vast country so great; it's the people
Who live here, our neighbors and friends,
These fellow Canadians make my life full!

And so I have to say a big "Thank You!"
And a huge "Happy Birthday!" as well,
To my dear country of choice, my Canada,
You, my friend, have treated me just swell!

Cataracts

What a weird word 'cataracts' is,
Makes me think of a waterfall,
Somewhere in the mountains,
Not inside a shopping mall.

But this word is a special one
For us with some eye concerns,
'Cuz it does hamper our vision,
Feeling like we've taken a bad turn!

Waiting almost a year, the day came,
Finally, I must say with glee,
My turn at the doctor, get this thing
Off my eye, so I can now see!

The foggy little membrane on my eye,
Was blurring my vision so bad,
But the doctor knew what to do,
In no time, cleaned up my eye pad.

Just a few minutes, it was over and done,
And I had a new lens in my eye,
Can't wait for the next to be done,
The colors are vivid—oh, my!

Lynda Horvath

Snowflakes

The snowflakes are falling,
It is as pretty as can be,
The sky has opened up wide,
So this beauty we can see!

Every snowflake is special,
Each has it's own fingerprint,
When they start to bunch up,
They make a nice winter hint!

These snowflakes are crispy,
They are as white as a ghost,
Even if you don't like winter,
Beautiful is snow a-top a post.

Sun shines above the clouds,
It is trying to peak through,
But snowflakes are more powerful,
And keep falling—so gently, too!

Soon the ground is all covered,
With beautiful shiny snowflakes,
That stay there till the sun shines,
They melt—that is all it really takes!

So while these snowflakes are falling,
We rejoice in their stunning beauty,
And enjoy the lovely picture they create
For all of us thankful folks to see!

My Friend, the Treadmill

Well, I have changed my tactics;
The old treadmill downstairs has called
To challenge me to walk on it
For (another) fifty-day challenge
To see what happens to my bod!
I started out slowly, just pacing
Carefully, and hanging on tight
As I jaunted along, at a 2.4 pace,
Reading as I walked,
To make the time go by quicker!
Fifteen minutes was my start,
To which you might laugh,
But it was a great start
For an old foggie like me,
Just starting out on this walking
Plan—fifty days of it, yet!!!
Soon I was up to seventeen minutes
At a time, three or four times a day!
Then I got brave and tried
Twenty minutes at a time!
And that is when it happened!!
I wasn't watching, slipped,

Lynda Horvath

Jerked my back and hip,
And the pain set in!
Some say to walk the pain out,
Some say to let it rest;
I continued to walk out the pain,
And it just got worse!
How much worse can it get?
OK, it is day 43, and I'm still here,
Giving this old treadmill a good
Work-out three times a day!
Do I feel better? Not sure!
But I do know, my new friend,
My treadmill, is still helping me
Trudging along!

The Moustache

I looked around and saw moustaches,
Sitting on faces, just above big smiles,
Why would anyone want such a thing,
Certainly not for me, not 'lady-styles'!

One moustache—speckled gray'ish-white,
Trimmed ever so carefully, hair by hair,
Just fits on his face, a perfect addition,
Can't ever imagine it not being there!

Moustaches seem to have a personality,
All of their very own—or so it does seem,
The fellow who owns this one is out-going,
He, Mr. R., is certainly a part of 'the team'!

Then there's another friendly moustache man,
He carefully trims and preens his with care,
This one is different—it has two handle-bars,
Mr. B. knows how to carefully wax it, hair by hair!

I think a moustache must be a lot of hard work,
To keep it looking nice, to keep every hair in place,
But I still do wonder why some men will choose,
To hide the nice skin that is on their cute face!

Lynda Horvath

Eagles

I knew very little about eagles, until today,
And that there are sixty species, they say.

The word 'eagle' means two different things,
Dark-colored and north-wind with wings!

The eagle, an 'endangered' species, it was,
It now is classed as 'threatened', just 'cuz.

The largest and most powerful bird of prey,
Wing span of over seven feet, they say.

And yet the smallest, weighing one pound,
You'd hardly know they are even around!

They're creatures of habit, forever do stay,
Where they were born, don't venture away.

Baby eaglets are well protected until they hatch,
Then fend for themselves, just one of a batch.

Twenty-five countries, on their coat of arms,
Have pictures of eagles, and all their charms.

The Native Americans, as part of their rites,
Use eagle feathers for various sights!

So, I've learned a few things about this bird,
Things I had never, ever, before read or heard.

Spider Webs!

This year, all around outside,
We seem to have spider webs,
That are clinging to everything
In sight—and they are huge!

So, in my wisdom, I thought
That I could get rid of them,
With my trusty watering hose
Using the most forceful setting.

I sprayed water from a distance,
I sprayed water up closer,
I sprayed water even closer yet,
I sprayed water directly upon them.

Not one bit of the web even moved,
Not one bit of the web came loose,
Not one bit, not one bit, at all,
So I had to literally pull them off!

What a surprise that was to me!
I had no idea that spider webs
Were so very strong, and clingy,
That they were just like glue!

Lynda Horvath

The spider worked so hard to create
This masterpiece, I tried to demolish
It with a hose—so unthoughtful of me
To extinguish this work of beauty.

A spider web shines in the sunlight,
It looks so pretty, some days,
But it messes up my pretty deck,
Makes me look like a bad deck-keeper.

So, sorry, little spider web on our deck,
You just have to be gone from here,
Find another place to spin your web,
Somewhere that loves you more than me!

Sleep!

It is three o'clock in the morning,
And I am wide, wide awake!
Can't get back to sleep again—
What on earth will it take?

The ducks, they are a-quacking,
Right outside our patio door,
They are a very noisy bunch,
"Please be quiet!" I implore!

Also right beside me in this room,
Is a guy who is snoring by my head,
He's getting louder and louder,
Can I please find another empty bed?

I've gone through the whole alphabet,
I've prayed for everyone from A to Zee,
I've searched the recesses of my mind,
And all I found was a clock, so tiny!

Well, now it is four o'clock on my watch,
An hour has quite slowly passed by,
I'm ready to sleep, that's not the issue—
If I could just shut at least one eye!

Lynda Horvath

It's now almost five o'clock in the morn,
Time to get the day on its merry way,
But I can't make very much noise just yet,
I'll awaken the snorer in my bed—not OK!

So, here I am—up, and sitting in the dark,
Writing this poem, looking for a good clue,
It is now as quiet as can be around here,
No ducks, no snores—what next shall I do?

This Sewing Machine

This sewing machine of mine,
I was ready to give away!
It worked for making placemats,
As many as eight in a day!

And then it started being bad,
The bobbin would not work,
So, after many hours of toil,
I said it must be 'Berzerk!'

So, I packed everything up,
The scissors, material, thread,
I packed them in big boxes,
And the machine, under a bed!

Well, as time went on, I thought
That maybe I should fix it,
As best I could, not a clue,
It was worth a try—bit by bit!

Lynda Horvath

So, I dug out my machine,
Threaded the complicated bobbin,
Found a piece of material,
Started—sounded like a robin!

Worked like a charm, that old thing,
Never skipped a thread or stitch,
Chirped right along, sooo great,
Even sewed without an itch!

So, now I have dug out all my stuff
That I can sew with such ease,
My machine just needed a rest,
Or, to me, it just wanted to tease.

Thank goodness I didn't throw
That silly machine out the door,
'Cuz now I can have some fun,
Placemats—I'll make some more!

Walking

Where shall we walk today?
The fountain, or
The crosswalk past the bridge, or
The food store, or
The drug store, or
The hotel down the street.

How many walks today?
For sure, one to the fountain, or
Just past the bridge, or
To the music jam.
Maybe two walks, to the bakery,
And, the fountain or bridge.

Lynda Horvath

Or, maybe three small walks,
As far as we think we can go.
Or, if it is a rainy day,
Or a very busy laundry day,
We might opt for no walks,
And just take a rest!

Whatever the case, we do try
To walk at least five thousand steps,
At a bare minimum, if we can.
Some days we walk seven or eight,
Thousand, that is,
And we are usually pooped!

Those China Cabinets!

I usually love the china in the cabinets,
But not so much today, it seems!
Every piece needs to be washed
The yearly job—not in my dreams!

Each piece needs attention, some water
They say--it will keep the china from cracks;
So, when I finish this poem, my lovely job—
Is to get busy, and wash them all--attack!

The plates, the cups, the saucers, the bowls,
The trays, the figurines, and the trinkets, too,
All need attention, all need a good soak,
It'll take me hours, but what else can I do?

As I wash each piece, it'll be like walking—
Walking down Memory Lane for each one,
Where did it come from? Who gave it to us?
Where will it go when we are all done?

So, five hours later, the job is complete,
I'm tired, but feeling so happy and content,
The china cabinets are clean and sparkly,
My bitter feelings—I never really meant!

Lynda Horvath

The Quick Lunches

Quick noon lunches
Are the very best!
No fuss, no muss,
Just have a rest!

Find some leftovers,
On the fridge shelf,
Just heat it up,
All by yourself!

Or noodle soup,
How quick is that,
Add some ketchup,
That has no fat!

Maybe some bread
With ham between,
Mustard and pickle,
But not baked bean!

Or just some dessert
Like a cinnamon bun,
Or two--heated,
Quickly that's done!

Lunch is so easy,
It's my favorite meal,
Takes no thought,
Just some food-appeal!

What's Important?

What is important in life? Is it all the trips you were able to take?
Is it how good you look? Or, the money you were able to make?

Is it how many friends you have? Or, is it the amount in your bank?
Is it the job you had? Or, is it someone you were able to thank?

Is it the family you were blessed with? Or, is it the color of your hair?
Is it the things you do for others? Or, is it that you really do care?

Whatever it is, nothing is more important in this troubled world today,
Than to love your family, friends~~and yourself~~in a very positive way!

Lynda Horvath

Little Things

It's the little things in life that mean the most;
It's often the little things about which we boast!

It's like the little rudder on a big, cruising boat,
That changes its course and keeps it afloat!

It's like the tiny little spark that helps a fire to start,
It continues to grow unless water squelches it apart!

It's like the little brick that starts to build a fireplace,
It sets the foundation~~a much-needed solid base!

It's our little tongue, and our little brain, that control what we say,
Whether the words be good or bad, whether it be night or day!

Windows

I should be washing windows, both inside and out,
The ones inside will be easy, there is no real doubt!

The ones outside, however, now look absolutely gross,
From the winter, snow, wind, and what-else~~who knows!

If it is warmer here tomorrow, I might try to venture outside,
With my vinegar and towel, and cleaning strokes real wide!

One thing I detest, is trying to clean windows without streaks;
I've never learned how~~I could do it for weeks and weeks . . .

And still not have nice, sparkly windows, no matter how hard I try;
I CAN still see through my dirty windows~~I'll just leave them~~sigh!

Lynda Horvath

Coloring Books

When I was a kid, coloring books were not often around,
They were too much of a luxury in our home to be found.

I loved to color at school~~the picture and the crayon,
Were all such a 'treat'~~I felt like I had definitely won!

So now I am older, and a coloring book I did buy,
For a couple of good reasons, I just cannot lie!

One of the reasons is to keep my mind alert and busy,
But little spaces, and keeping inside the lines~~I'm dizzy!

The other reason is to keep my hands nimble and strong,
I think I will just color tomorrow~~all the colorful day long!

Yard Work

Working in the yard can be so very much fun;
Cleaning the flower beds~~now they are done!

The weeds are pulled, the soil has had a good turn,
The lawn has been mowed, and the muscles are a-burn,

Why is this old body so creaky and sore today?
I used to do the whole yard at once, and it was OK!

I guess I'm showing my age, as sad as that can be,
I'm going to play my iPad, that agrees with me!

Lynda Horvath

The Cold

So, it has happened,
The day of 'the cold'
Has already arrived,
In mid-September,
The second day of fall,
With the loud sneezes,
And the irritating sniffles,
And the raspy throats,
And the horrible feelings,
That come with this dread.

So, off to the drug store,
Lozenges by the package,
Cough drops by the dozen,
To, hopefully, stop this
Plague from spreading to others.
Don't feel like eating,
Don't feel like talking,
Don't feel like doing anything,
Just want to relax and rest,
This sick body of mine!

Hopefully, within a day or so
This dreaded 'friend' will leave
Our bodies in search of some place
Else, anywhere would be good!
Neither of us have had a cold
For many, many years,
So I guess it is our turn
To just let this thing run
Its course in our bodies,
And hope it is soon gone!

The Wind Storm of 2017

The wind and the rain~~how necessary they both are!
If we didn't have wind, the leaves wouldn't go far!
The trees would stay stuffed with dry leaves and twigs,
And they would start to look just ugly and very big!

The wind we had last night, made our backyard a war zone;
There were more leaves and twigs and branches, not alone,
Mainly from the big, huge tree next door—and many-a cone ;
Took a big, long clean-up to see, each nice patio stone.

Lots of wind damage done within our city limits,
With this hundred-seven kilo an hour wind blast,
We were all so glad when the wind called it quits!
Now, it is merely a spring event of the past!

Lynda Horvath

Coffee

Our coffee is important to us, that we do know,
We like it in the morning, to get our blood a-flow!
Then mid-morning, while watching 'Let's Make a Deal',
Oh, yes! It is a good, refreshing, stimulating feel!

We like our special coffee, we thought it was cheap,
But last store visit, we found a new kind to keep!
We used to make a pot of coffee for fifty odd cents,
Now it's half that~~keep this one!~~it makes sense!

We hardly drink booze, we don't have many vices,
Don't eat extravagantly, or use too many spices!
We'll keep enjoying our coffee, that we will just do,
For experts now say~~'Coffee is sooo good for you!'

The Day Before

Why is it so hard to wait for a special date?
You book a nice trip, then you have to wait!

It's fun to plan, to research, and find something new,
As well as find something interesting that you can do!

You clean the house, mow the lawn, and pack your bag,
Hope you haven't forgotten anything~~someone might nag!

The night before, you cannot seem to sleep,
Even if you count ten thousand odd sheep!

It's here, the time~~the time has finally come;
Thank goodness your great planning is all done!

Lynda Horvath

Traveling

We have travelled by Shank's pony, by car, by bus, by train,
By cruise ship; but the best and quickest is definitely by plane!

To get from here to there, if it is too far or too hard to walk,
One must figure the very best way to get around the block!

Shank's pony got me to school until the school bus came by,
The school bus worked until the end of high school did fly!

Shank's pony again in Edmonton to work, and then back to school;
With two boys, with no car to get around--I must have been a fool!

Finally, a car to get around this huge, big city,
For us, that really was something quite pretty!

Then, for trips away from here, there came the plane,
A cruise ship was next, and finally came the train!

How lucky we are, in this day and age, to travel so well,
If one type doesn't work, there's others to choose--swell!

Congratulations!

Change is very hard to accomplish, no matter what it is,
It's even harder when it is a major part of your life's biz!

Little by little, with a lot of great effort, a change can be made,
Before you know it, you've made a few gains up the change-grade!

Quitting smoking is a very tough one, I have watched it happen here,
In our household, with lots of trials, but support always very near!

One week gone, two weeks gone, now one month, then two,
Now we've reached one hundred days smoke-free--ya-hoo!

What an accomplishment, we are all so proud of what you've done,
In our books, you're a hero, a trooper--you're absolutely number one!

Two men in our little family have become great heroes this year,
They have persevered, they have been determined--soooo dear!

So, sincere ' Congratulations!' to these two dear folk,
Your life will be better, cleaner, and sweeter--no joke!

Lynda Horvath

Canada 150!

People in Canada are celebrating 150 years post-Confederation,
This July first, right across our ten provinces--our great nation!
What can we be proud of, as Canadian citizens, that we can proclaim,
Without grumbling about politics--let's see how many things I can name.

Mountains and waterfalls, prairie fields and rolling hills, blue-green lakes,
Rocky cliffs and rushing rivers, oceans on either side, even snowflakes;
Busy cities, small towns, huge grain operations, even a small family farm,
Big cattle farms, high-rises, parks--all part of Canada's wonderful charm!

Four great seasons, each we can enjoy in their own climatic way,
Spring with its new growth and burst of color, Summer--by day,
The heat and beauty around us, Fall's gorgeous colors burst out,
Winter's snowfalls--sometimes we just want to shovel and shout!

A plethora of different ethnic foods, people and customs galore,
Canada has become a melting pot of nations--a mosaic, no bore!
There are many more reasons Canada needs to be celebrated, for sure,
I guess that's why this country has been able--for 150 years--to endure!

Rainbows

I just looked out our window, and what did I find?
I found a rainbow--a very bright, colorful kind!

The colors, who ever thought of them--ROY G. BIV;
At the end of it, a pot of gold--that would help us live!

The Red for shiny apples, the Orange for bright tulips,
These top colors of the rainbow resemble cow-slips.

The Yellow for lemons, the Green for freshly-cut grass,
The middle colors of the rainbow give it some class.

The Blue for the afternoon sky, Indigo for a blue-green lake,
These bottom colors are what help keep us alert and awake.

And then there is Violet, the purple color on the very bottom,
What a beautiful, colorful ark in the rainy sky--it's no 'Ho, Hum'!

Lynda Horvath

Coffee Update!

We bought a new kind of coffee—much, much cheaper
Than the kind we had been using--would it be a keeper?

After many pots of coffee, after giving it a fair 'try'
We made a decision, one that would surprise us--sigh!

The coffee seems to taste like dish-water, most days,
The 'zing' of the flavor is sometimes there, not always!

We've increased the strength, we've lessened the cream,
We both were almost ready for a big, huge, loud scream!

As I said in the 'coffee' poem before, our vices--really quite few,
So why are we scrimping on decent coffee--ain't that a clue?

So, we cleaned out the coffee pot, got rid of the cheap stuff,
Filled it with our good coffee--again--that's good enough!

Our experiment is over, we've learned a small lesson in drinks,
Be happy with what you have, 'cuz cheaper isn't all one thinks!

Coffee, coffee, we do love you two (or three) times a day,
We can just sit and relax, play our iPads, or just sip away!

Our Backyard

It's the beginning of July, and we are enjoying our pots
Of plants in the back yard--there are a few, not lots!

But what we do have, they are doing very, very well,
Out of the pots and barrels, they just seem to swell!

The colors are lovely, they are mixing and matching so great
All around the patio, from the fountain in the corner to each gate!

Even the tomatoes and herbs, something a bit new for us this year,
Are doing their best to give us a reason, or two, to spread cheer!

The perennials, the best they have ever been in our back yard,
Are blooming, and spreading--they could be on a picture card!

I must get out there, right now, and give them some fertilizer and a drink,
Because I sure don't want them to think of shriveling up, or to shrink!

It's my hope that I can keep them looking pretty, and nice, all summer long,
And into September--so a bit of extra TLC, and things shouldn't go wrong.

This might seem boastful, but it really just shows, that with a bit of hard work--
A relaxing, pretty, colorful, plant-filled patio and backyard is a nice perk!

Lynda Horvath

Cinnamon Buns

I have finally learned how to make cinnamon buns in the bread-maker,
Such an easy task to do--milk, water, marg, sugar, salt from the shaker.

Then an egg, flour and yeast go into the bread-maker's mixing pan,
Turn it on for ninety minutes--a lovely lump of dough for you to scan!

Pat it, roll it--some cinnamon and brown sugar, and maybe a nut or two,
Make a long roll, cut it up into pieces, let the dough rise--no more to do!

Well, except to put your pan in the oven, let it bake for a third of an hour,
And you cannot resist one--or two--you will have absolutely no will-power!

They are fun to make, especially when you can share them with friends;
They are great around a campfire, a nice gift to someone on-the-mend!

In Osoyoos, they kept the motel admin happy, as well as the neighbors, too,
Everyone thinks they take a lot of time to make--they are really easy to do!

So, I will just keep making them, 'cuz everyone seems to enjoy them so much,
I might try to vary my recipe a bit, just to give them a different palate-touch!

They smell so good, coming out of the oven--sweet, crusty, and yummy,
I think I had better go make a batch, or two--to fill up my empty tummy!

Storms

They said a bad storm was coming this afternoon,
With hail, wind, rain--the TV said it would be soon!

They even warned our area of the chance of a nasty tornado,
We lived through one thirty years ago--not nice--we know!

So, we moved our plants into the garage--those we could,
Because they are so nice right now, protect them--we should!

We watched the skies all afternoon, a drizzle of rain came down,
It got dark, cloudy, a tiny bit windy--nothing more hit this town!

We decided to leave the plants safe in the garage tonight, to be sure,
For one never knows what a night of weather might bring up or stir!

By morning, nothing had changed--we had no storm, rain or hail,
The plants had a nice evening in the garage, in their pots and pail!

Lynda Horvath

Picture Albums

There are a couple of jobs that I have needed to do for a while,
One is to go through a bunch of old pictures, some in a big pile!

Sorted--kept some, got rid of some--cropped, mounted and more,
Made up one album, but needed another two--off to the store!

More cutting and pasting, now three full picture albums are done,
An emotional trip through Memory Lane--a great deal of personal fun!

There still is a pile of pictures--what should I do with them, I ask;
My 'album' goal has been to have no mess for the kids--a task!!!

Just keep things that are important, that will mean something one day,
To those left behind, less to dump and junk--that should be okay!

Family pictures are special, if you know who they are, and how related to you,
Let's keep the important, meaningful ones--the people each of us knew!

Fires

On the TV this week--lots of terrible, horrible BC fire news,
People all over the continent sending lots of helping crews.

The devastation already, is almost more than one can imagine,
But the live pictures on TV certainly leave nothing to fathom.

People have lost homes, pets, treasures and all personal stuff,
Life going forward for them--it will certainly be very, very rough!

We've seen tragic fires before in Ft. McMurray and Slave Lake,
People fleeing their homes, with the few things they can take!

It must be an awful feeling, seeing smoke and flames coming near,
The skies overhead are filled with black smoke--not at all clear!

Fleeing on roads full of backed-up vehicles, some moving very slow,
Hearts pounding fast, unsure of life, not even knowing where to go!

Wondering if your home will be safe--will you be able to return some day?
All of these thoughts cloud your mind as you journey, from the fire, away!

No end in sight--the news is still very bad--the fire continues to rage,
It's a lot to process, a lot to worry about--regardless of your age!

Lynda Horvath

Crosswords

I have found (another) way to waste my most-valuable time,
It's exciting, it's using my brain, and it doesn't cost a dime!

A friend shared about the thirty crosswords he checks each day,
He said it keeps his brain active, creating a new word to (maybe) say!

So, on my iPad, I downloaded a puzzle--had so much fun--needed more,
I can see why my friend has so many--life, with crosswords--is never a bore!

Some words I have never heard of, like **na, jo, rete, rez** and **odea,**
And, **oe** or **cox** (along with other weird ones) just blow me away!

I'm learning some new words, don't known how to use them to make sense,
Don't know if there are past, present or future--don't know their tense!

All-in-all, this new iPad app is keeping me really quite busy--when I want,
It's challenging my brain, making me think, so I have new words to flaunt!

So, I had better get back to my crosswords, all sixteen at this time,
Forget this poem, 'cuz I can't think of another thing to make rhyme!

Craving...

I have a craving for borscht--my favorite kind of soup,
Just can't wait to have a big spoonful--maybe a scoop!

Went to Safeway, bought some beets, carrots, a tater or two,
Came home, chopped them up, all boiling in a pot--who knew?

Next into the mix--an onion and some garlic sausage, too,
Parsnips, spices--beginning to look like a nice big stew!

It simmered and boiled, and simmered some more, it smelled great,
We both were drooling--for supper, we just could not possibly wait!

So, at four o'clock, with a big bowl, some crackers, and sour cream,
We gobbled down a big, big bowl--it totally fulfilled my 'soup' dream!

The best thing about this meal, 'cuz that really was what it became,
I took out all the calories, so if we get fatter--the soup's not to blame!

Lynda Horvath

Sittin' on the Deck

Sittin' on the deck at ten in the morn,
Not a single cloud in the sky overhead,
Just the sound of a distant car horn,
And the delicious waft of rising bread!

With a mug of steaming coffee in my hand,
Surrounded by pretty flowers--pink and red,
Watching the bees--on the flowers they land,
Beautiful summery things, from 'eh' to 'zed'!

Now the sound of a lawn-mower doing its work,
Making the grass nice around a flower bed,
Nice to have a well-trimmed yard--a perk,
"I like your neat yard!" the neighbors said!

Summer is short, enjoy every day while you can,
Fresh air will boost your spirits, clear your head,
Whether on the deck, or getting a nice sun tan,
Enjoy these warm, sunny months--fall is ahead!

Stressed Friends

We have some dear friends who seem to be going through a lot of stress,
They are persevering as best they can--determined their life won't be a mess!

One friend has recently had a cancer-related surgery--not fun,
Now spouse for surgery, not looking forward to his bladder re-done!

Another friend's Mom has cancer in many different places in her bod,
And her Dad now has dementia real bad--her time will need a nod!

One more friend is selling a house, buying another, starting a new job,
With the spouse leaving a job, finding another--ahead of the mob!

One friend couple is still grieving the loss of an only son years ago,
Their life changed that day, and their hearts are still filled with woe.

Lynda Horvath

Yet another friend recently lost her husband of thirty-some years,
Will she have to move? What will life bring now? Lots of fears!

Trying to deal with retirement is a trial another friend seems to face,
Depression, sadness, lack of energy--happiness? Not a trace!!

Three boys, all under six, so busy my dear friend is these days,
A year away from the classroom--time for lots of boy-time plays!

I could add more names--how often we take life for granted, how sad,
Make the most of each day, the most of each opportunity--be glad!

People

People are the folk you meet,
Either when you are alone or with someone;
Often they are ones you greet,
Perhaps after a long day of work is done;
Laughing together on the street,
Exclaiming to them while having some fun!

People are the folk you are related to,
Each of them has their own agenda and life;
Often it is different, you have no clue,
Positively trying to avoid any unnecessary strife;
Letting daily life just be so good to you,
Enjoying every day with your husband or wife!

People are the folk you have not met yet,
Each of them going down an exciting road;
Oddly enough, they may be from a familiar set,
Playing their cards right, with not a heavy load;
Listening for clues that for you are a sure bet,
Expecting to meet you, in your, or their, abode!

Lynda Horvath

People are some folks you wish you had not met,
Experiences you had, you never would have thought;
Often putting you in situations where the bar was set,
Perhaps feeling like a fish, and that you were caught;
Lessons were learned, your life became stronger yet,
Each challenge, an experience that couldn't be bought!

People are folks you already have as a great friend,
Excited to share life with you, through thick and thin;
Often there for you, at a beginning and at an end,
Positively helping you, every hard obstacle to win;
Looking out for you, around each and every bend,
Enthusiastically helping you through life's constant spin!

Saskatoons

We got a phone call, an invite to pick
Some saskatoons at a friend's farm,
So we got ourselves ready real quick
And ventured to the country~~no harm!

We found the berry patch, it was very big
And the berries were even bigger still;
We marveled at the berry patch~~like figs,
So our gallon-or-so pail we began to fill.

Less than an hour later~~no room left in the pail,
So we quickly drove home to get busy here,
To clean and wash and baggie our berry-bail,
Fourteen two-cup baggies~~that's not mere!

Into the freezer, most of those baggies were seen,
For the muffins and desserts during the cold;
Today saskatoon pudding, tarts, on ice cream,
Just shows~~picking berries~~you're never too old!

Lynda Horvath

Well-Witching

These words seem like such a big joke!
Who ever heard of such, regarding a well?
We were reminded during a visit with folk,
That such an activity can turn out swell!

At home on the farm, we tried to find water,
It was a never-ending plight for all of us;
We dug and dug, quicksand a big bother,
It threw us under the moving big bus!

We hired a water-witcher~~a man with a great gift,
Some people just thought we were nuts;
But when he found the spot~~the water did lift,
Right to the surface and more~~tut-tut!

Those people were fooled, and water we did finally get,
Especially great 'cuz into the farm house it did arrive,
And to quench the thirst of every farm animal and pet,
We all were happy—and we even felt more alive!

So, the way you find water is a bit different today,
But sixty years ago, this method was quite in use;
We take water for granted, so often, each day,
But when you don't have it, it seems like abuse!

I loved our water wells on the farm, though hard to get,
The old pump was a treat to use, but very tough to work;
Water~~the substance of life, the best way to get wet,
When you feel thirsty, a little drink of it is quite a perk!

Silence

Today we heard about **silence**--a huge lack in our lives,
We are always too busy, long past the nines to fives!

There is the lawn to mow, the weeds are always waiting,
Housework--always there--has an exaggerated rating!

We could go shopping, we could clean a cupboard or two,
We could vacuum the van, or sweep the deck, on cue!

We might read a book, walk in the mall--what can we see?
Write in our daily journal, or listen to something on TV!

Do any of these bring 'silence' where your mind is free?
Absolutely free of noise, distractions, anything we see?

Silence, something I do not know how to achieve or do,
I always feel I need to be busy--from my head to my shoe!

So, my goal is this to try: no books, no TV, no noise, no one,
Nothing but my mind and me--sitting--alone--having fun!

It cannot be a sin to be idle, to just let your mind flow free,
Forget the busyness of life--just my empty mind and me!

"Silence is a great source of strength," they say,
And, "silence is a true friend who will never betray!"

Lynda Horvath

August!

Well, here we have a new month--the eighth this year,
Seven months have completely passed--in the rear!

It's the middle of summer, that seems to be our fear,
The days will soon get shorter--that's what we hear!

It's been a great spring and summer, we enjoy with a peer,
Whether at home or away, the sunshine is usually near!

And if the sun is not shining, the lovely rain can be so clear,
Making the grass and plants so green--we cannot sneer!

What will this beautiful summer month bring us--oh, dear,
As we work at playing, and play at working--life in gear!

We know we'll have fun, whatever we do, without a tear,
'Cuz we'll walk through August together, with no fear!

Mushrooms

Mushrooms--they always taste so good with steak,
Or in a stew, with pork chops, or maybe a cake!

Mushroom bread, that sounds like a good thing to bake,
To eat at home, or, on a summer day, to take to the lake!

However, there are mushrooms in our lawn, they are not fake,
Because all over our front grass, they've seemed to over-take!

We get out there, pull them when the soil is moist, or use a rake,
Trying hard to get rid of them, for our neighborhood's sake!

We'll keep trying, our nice mushroom-less grass we'll try to make,
So the front yard looks nice, when we go to sleep or when we wake!

Lynda Horvath

Our World Today

It's a scary world these days
As we watch the happenings on TV,
As we hear the daily breaking news,
And talk to our concerned friends.

Some people seem to dominate the news
With their useless tweets and shenanigans;
Some people seem to feel that their opinions
Are the only ones that need to be heard!

So what is the best thing to do today?
How can you turn off the TV and become
Oblivious to all this world-nonsense-garbage,
Trying to think it is not happening?

Well, what I'm going to do today is this:
I'm going to try to watch less TV, read more
Fun books, write more positive poems,
And pray for a complete world at peace!

Scrabble

I've started playing this new game on my iPad--Scrabble,
It causes me to make words that I wouldn't even babble!

Words I have never heard of, show up in the dictionary,
So I just use them when I can--need those points to carry!

Some folks are very, very good at this well-known word game,
Make great words, get points--they actually put me to shame!

Most are so much better than me, I am not afraid to admit,
Every day I learn a new word--someday they are bound to fit!

At any given time, I've got twenty-five crossword puzzles on the go,
So during the day, a few minutes at a time, creative juices can flow!

I like my new game--it keeps my mind busy, it keeps my brain a-movin',
Maybe someday I'll get thirty crossword buddies--just keep a-groovin'!

Lynda Horvath

Why Am I So Lazy?

I'm having another struggle with housework,
It just does not seem very important to me;
I used to fuss and fume, the dust never to lurk,
Spending endless hours--for no one else to see.

No one comes to visit, just to see if your dust is gone,
They would never notice the un-vacuumed rug,
Or the full laundry basket, or all the dishes not done--
But, they might notice the lack of a soft, sweet hug!

Although trying to always keep our house tidy and neat,
Is important to us--always ready if the doorbell might ring,
Something nice to nibble on, coffee that can't be beat,
A comfy place to sit--now we can just listen to you sing!

So, come on over--the door is open wide, waiting for you,
Our friendly house is as clean as my 'lazy self' has done;
We're always ready for company, even if the sky isn't blue,
And, if you're lucky, there will be a fresh, hot cinnamon bun!

Summer!

I'm sitting here cooking--the sun this morning is so very hot,
It's ten o'clock, and I almost need to move to a cooler spot!

There's a bit of a breeze, which does seem to help some,
But I need to enjoy this sunshine, before summer is done!

My coffee cup is full of a steaming freshly-brewed treasure,
And I can just sit here--enjoying the colorful flowers--my pleasure!

The leaves on the big trees are starting to turn, from green to yellow,
The geese overhead, some going north, some south--confused fellow!

There's smoke in the air, making the sun a bright orangish-red,
There's not a single white fluffy cloud in the vast sky overhead!

Oh, how I love a day like this, nature's beauty at its very, very best,
No matter where I look, there is beauty--north, south, east or west!

One must make the most of every day, regardless of the weather,
I can't help but love this one--the sights, sounds, and smell of heather!

Lynda Horvath

Life-long Friendships

Friendships today can be complicated and hard,
Everyone is so busy, tending to life or their yard!

Not everyone wants to give up valuable time or stuff,
To just meet for a coffee, or share life off-the-cuff!

What keeps relationships strong, is to just keep in touch,
With a phone call, a text, a quick visit--doesn't have to be much!

Some of my friends I see maybe once or twice during a year,
But we always know each other is 'there'--always quite near!

We could just pick up the phone, we could be there in an hour,
Regardless of circumstances, nothing is beyond our friend-power!

Some friends we see often, cultivating precious memories each time,
Those get-togethers are priceless, sharing life experiences at their prime!

Oh, I'm thankful for friends, some are far away, some are very near,
Regardless of distance, each one will always be held very dear!

My oldest friend, I've known for sixty-six awesome years--how sweet,
My youngest friend--I just met last week--getting to know them, a treat!

Up's and Down's!

Life--the up's and down's of life can be overwhelming, for sure;
Walking through them with your head held high--hard to endure!

The up's can be wonderful, you feel such a sense of delight,
It can keep you on cloud nine from early morning until late at night!

The many up's will encourage you, your life on a huge upward swing,
Everything is like sweet, beautiful roses, and you just want to loudly sing!

If our short life was all up's, I really wonder how happy we would be,
It might unlock every door we faced, especially if we have the right key!

Unfortunately, one is often handed the other side of life--the down's!
They can quickly upset your apple cart, and cause many, many frowns!

Sometimes the lack of money can make your life turn upside down,
So you must work a little harder, change that cash from green to brown!

Sometimes the loss of someone very special can create a horrible state,
You find yourself thinking that you just have too much on your life-plate!

Lynda Horvath

Relationships can cause some down's in your life, too, very sad to say,
You can work really hard to keep them positive, but there's just no way!

One of my greatest up's was holding my first grandchild in my arms,
She looked so sweet and innocent, such red hair, full of charms!

My biggest of down's in my life was identifying my dear son, at his death,
Even today, so many years later, that event still takes away my breath!

Luckily, in my life, I have had more memorable up's than I've had down's,
For which I am most thankful--smiles are easier to spread than frowns!

So, for the many future up's and down's that are left in my lifetime,
May I handle them with grace and love, and continue to rhyme!

Amazing Geese!

As we sat on the deck, watching the geese fly one evening this week,
We wondered why, in September, they were flying north--just taking a peek?

And then we read that they often 'stage' together with many more,
To have a good feed before they fly safely from some lakeshore.

They fly in a 'V' formation, with one in the lead, until the leader gets too tired,
Then the leader falls back into the formation, and lets another become hired!

With flying in such a formation, the uplift for the geese right behind,
Creates a seventy-one percent greater flying range--a very helpful kind!

The geese at the back are noisy, as we could hear down here on the ground,
They constantly honk, to encourage all the others at the front and all around!

When one gets out of the formation, it is very hard for them to fly alone,
So they quickly get back into the 'V' to help them get to their final home!

Lynda Horvath

If one of the geese in the flock becomes hurt or just too weak to fly,
Two other geese leave the group, stay with the one that is hurt--why?

They take care of each other--when one is hurt, two are there to assist,
Until the hurt bird is feeling better, and once again able to fly--to persist!

The migration route can vary, from three to seven thousand miles,
They can travel up to fifteen hundred miles on a good day--all smiles!

Geese are like people in so many ways, especially their advanced teamwork,
We can learn so much from them about working together, not expecting a perk!

Helping one another, sharing life's load, being patient, helping take the lead,
Let's be like those amazing geese, let's keep in touch with each other's need!

September Weather

September's weather in Edmonton--it can be hard to predict,
You are not sure what to expect--which season will be picked?

Some September days were so very warm--in fact, really very hot,
Lounging on the deck--that did really hit the best relaxing spot.

Some days were a bit rainy, even a bit of cold hail came down,
But it didn't last here very long, in this northern Alberta town.

Other September days were just nice, very easy to really enjoy,
But the nights--some of them were very cool--just to annoy!

Regardless of the weather, the leaves are just gorgeous and stunning,
One can't get enough of the amazing colors--unless you are running!

The reds, yellows, oranges, browns, and different shades of green,
Leaves, in this season, are always the prettiest you've ever seen!

This is one of my very favorite months of the calendar year--September,
It marks the end of summer, it can be enjoyed before the cold of winter.

So, the various weathers of September--I've learned to fully enjoy,
Just take each day as it happens--treat it like a brand new toy!

Lynda Horvath

Flowers

The flowers outside have done so very well this year!
They blossomed, bloomed and have been beautiful here!

They have taken lots of work--the fertilizer, the water, the care,
Each and every day, without fail, not a drop of plant-love to spare!

We've enjoyed these flowers, they've brightened up each and every day,
From May through to September, at least--like a sunshine's sunny ray!

And now, we have had a few cold days in our flower garden at the back,
And the plants are looking a bit droopy, they've lost their perky knack!

They've had enough of looking pretty, just for our very grateful eyes,
They've created so much happiness all these months--how time flies!

So, within the next ten days, before the snow decides to coat the ground,
We will probably have to remove our plants--they won't be around!

Always sad to do, it is the end of another great season of the year,
A time to reflect, a time to gather thoughts, maybe even shed a tear!

Now we can plan for next spring--what grew well, what didn't do well,
'Cuz we know next summer, our flowers, again, will look just swell!

Our Office!

The office in our house is a relaxing place to spend some time,
Two nice big windows let in the sunshine, if up the stairs I climb!

It's a great place to write some poems, in my lovely new book,
Poems about everything from mowing the grass to having to cook.

Another thing I do in that room is color in my adult coloring book,
Stay in the lines, match the colors, be creative--by hook or by crook!

'My Memoirs'--what a great spot to contemplate my life's journeys so vast,
To be able to write, and remember, many experiences from my past!

Or just to sit and read, in that nice warm, sunny room--by the hour,
Could be a story about history, a biography, or even about a flower!

I would miss that cozy room, if I didn't still live here in this place,
I spend a lot of time in there--it is my very favorite space!

Lynda Horvath

Peace of Mind

Can anyone have a true sense of 'peace of mind' today?
In this world of ours, it is a hard task to trust and obey.

Sometimes you are tricked and made to look like a fool,
It often happens in adult life, too, not only in a school!

Sometimes one's thoughts sadly take a negative turn,
And it's hard to relate to others--a lesson to learn!

It's a continual work-in-progress, this peace-of-mind stuff,
It doesn't happen, or come easily--sometimes it's quite rough!

Having a strong faith helps my peace of mind,
Being honest, trustworthy, reliable and kind!

It also comes from knowing what's right,
And trying my best to 'fight the good fight!'

Clouds

Clouds come in all shapes and sizes--some fluffy, some sleek,
They can look so far away, or they can look so very close;
I'm looking at some now--shapes from cat to mountain peak,
Then they change from fluffy tree to a petal-ly white rose!

Above the clouds, in a plane, is quite a different kind of scene,
You're sitting on those fluffy, white clouds, or going through them,
Can't see a thing--surrounded by whiteness, fluffy, so serene,
Each individual cloud like a little hidden, yet special, gem!

Lying on your back on the grass, looking at the different shapes,
Trying to figure what some of those clouds might look like,
Is it Roy Rogers on Tonto, or is it Batman with a long cape?
Or maybe it's an angel, keeping you from riding a bike!

Those clouds are meant to protect you from the vast sky above,
Unless there's a storm brewing, and the clouds will turn dark,
Regardless, each one is full of joy, peace, compassion and love!
Enjoy these wonders of the universe--like watching a fire's spark!

Lynda Horvath

Clay

Our lives are like a chunk of clay~~hard, but pliable, dull but unique;
As a child we are molded~~by our parents, family and even antiques!

As we grow up, we are shaped by people with whom we spend time;
As we become adults, we continue to be formed, with a bit of grime!

Experiences of life, like the clay shaped by the hands of the potter,
The speed life turns, like the potter's wheel and some water!

In Tucson we saw a potter at work, choosing a life from riches to rags;
He transformed a hunk of clay into a beautiful piece, with priceless tags!

He shared that his vase had many nicks, imperfections and flaws,
But it was a gorgeous, one-of-a-kind, piece of art~~just because!

He likened it to our lives; none of us are perfect, all with scars from living,
Each piece a beautiful masterpiece, shaped by~~for others~~our giving!

I must keep working on this old, withered chunk of hard clay,
In hopes it will be soft, beautiful and meaningful, some fine day!

Gettin' Old!

This business of **gettin' old** can be not so very nice!
Some days it's not much fun to roll this 'senior' dice!

Your hair has turned a number of different colors--gray/white,
And the oomph in your step has taken a vacation to the right!

Your limp and your shuffle, thanks to arthritis in those bones,
Makes you take walks a little slower, with many more moans!

It takes you longer to clean your house, or to even pull weeds,
And suppers for two--just not the same delicious healthy feeds!

Lynda Horvath

However, despite all that physical stuff that everyone can see,
Your still have your spark and ambition--it hasn't seemed to flee!

On most days, your get-up-and-go has got-up-and-went,
But you are so thankful for the wonderful days you have spent!

There are many more wonderful days to come, each you will enjoy,
New experiences, too, enjoyed just like getting a brand new toy!

Getting' old--it really is just a matter of perception--often not so right,
It's really just what you make it—by delightful day or even by night!

So, limpy and crickety, moany and sore, gray/white hair—who cares?
I'm still walking around, enjoying life, laughing lots, as I walk up stairs!

Life's Blessings

Life's many blessings--something we really do not understand,
Until we have been faced with complications right at our hand!

Do we understand hunger? Have we had to miss a delicious meal?
We have loads of food in our cupboards—none we have had to steal!

Do we understand cold? Have we had to sleep on the dark, lonely street?
No, we have blankets and comforters to warm us from our head to our feet!

Do we understand loneliness--not knowing a soul to talk to at anytime?
Family and friends—we have many, who would come to us on a dime!

Do we understand freedom of speech? Do we have to guard what we say?
No, we are able to share our thoughts and feelings aloud, each and every day!

Lynda Horvath

Do we understand persecution? Can we worship as we want, any time?
Our choice of churches, faith-base, religious convictions~~at a prime!

Do we understand poverty? No where to lay our head at night? No money?
Many of us have been poor in our lives, but a little cash is like sweet honey!

One could go on and on, with listing all our blessings by the huge ton,
When we stop and think of all we have, we really know we have won!

We have won the race, no matter how much we have, no matter our age,
But sometimes we need to remind ourselves with a question on our life-page!

Are we grateful? Do we take all we enjoy for granted? Are our priorities right?
Daily, we must count our blessings—there are so many—from morning till night!

My Classmate

It was September, 1951, when I met my new classmate;
Over sixty years later, it is great, with her family, to go on a date!

Little did we know, as we walked three miles to school together,
Up-hill both ways, in absolutely all kinds of great Alberta weather ...

That we would become, and stay, friends for many long years to come;
We walked through rain, sunshine, snow drifts till our toes were numb!

We argued, we fought, we laughed, we cried, we even got in trouble,
By sitting and playing a game, after a three-mile walk, trouble-double!

Sometimes we rode our bikes, sometimes the coal trucks gave us a ride,
But from the senior boys, on that long walk we could not seem to hide!

They knew how to frighten us, they knew that two little girls could not run,
So they tormented and teased, they bullied us, too--until we were DONE!

Finally, the bus came in about Grade Five, we were so thankful, for sure,
Caught it at seven o'clock, back home at five, a very long day to endure!

We were the first two families on in the morning, the very last off at night,
We certainly had lots of times for visiting, games, and often a good fight!

Lynda Horvath

Somehow we all managed to complete our schooling, at our dear alma mater,
And went our separate ways--jobs, university, marriage, kids--a teeter-totter!

Years went by, we saw one another a few times, even though we lived close by,
Our Grade Twelve fiftieth anniversary--planning that together, sealed the tie!

We regularly get together, as couples we have a lot of good, clean fun,
We can visit, holiday, drink wine, tell stories--we never seem to be done!

It will be sixty-six years next week, since we started school in Grade One;
I hope we have many more years of friendship, kinship, laughter and fun!

'Pick-Up' Friends

Some friends--you can just 'pick-up' from the last visit with them,
And carry on sharing your lives together--they are a definite gem!

We can catch up on the latest news of each kid and grandkid,
Where each one of them are, and what each one of them did!

Stories--some of them funny, some of them sad--easily flow,
Just cementing our relationship together--why? Do we know?

Well, what we do know, it's always been so very loud and clear,
We're all the kind of friends who, for each other, we loudly cheer!

We have each other's back, whether we see each other often or not,
We'd do anything to help the other--that's what we've been taught!

So, these special friends we visited today, we've known for over forty years,
Have been our partners through many happy times, and even through tears!

Friends like these are valued beyond anything else one could wish to possess,
We look forward to many more years of 'sharing life together'--OH, YES, YES!

Lynda Horvath

Silence is Golden

'Silence is golden'--a saying we have heard for many years,
It is something dearly lacking in our lives, as a busy life appears!

The TV takes over our family rooms, blaring endlessly away,
Making that comfy room--not the greatest place to stay!

If it isn't the television, it's the radio, or a loud music machine,
Hate to admit it, but all three of these--I'm not really that keen!

Silence, that beautiful lost art, unless we take a very firm stand,
And create some time of silence in our lives, walking hand in hand.

Silence can be deafening--silence can be intimidating, as well,
It can be uncomfortable, but, most importantly, it can be swell!

Some of your best thinking can take place when your mind is free,
Free of all that clutters, free of busy thoughts--it rarely can be!

Love my times of silence, they mean so much to me as I get older,
I'll make a list of future things to contemplate--in my 'Silence' folder!

Every Person Has a Story

Just heard this staying on TV, relating to a life well-spent,
'Every person has a story'--no matter the direction they went!

Everyone has done special things is their life--woman or gent,
Gone places they never would imagine--worth more than a cent!

The story may share happy times, like summer camping in a tent,
Or finding out that someone anonymously paid your monthly rent!

The story may share sad times, like your brand new car has a dent,
Or, after falling on the icy sidewalk, your broken arm is badly bent.

Whatever the story, each will be unique and personally well-meant,
And maybe to the local newspaper, they should really be sent!

The story doesn't have to be glamorous, or even about where you went,
Just about living life to the fullest, with lots of fun times, lady or gent!

Lynda Horvath

Stars in the Sky

Stars in the sky can be so invisible
In the city, as we try to get to sleep,
They're over-powered by streetlights,
So to the sky, we cannot even peep!

We know the twinkling stars are hiding up there
In the big, vast, fluffy sky that is over-head,
But we cannot really see them at all,
As we try to get to sleep in our comfy bed.

However, out in the country, with no streetlights,
With no house porch light or a headlight from a car,
The twinkly, sparkly, shimmering lights in the sky;
What lit up our bedroom? Why, a bright, shiny star!

The lone North Star shone brilliantly, as did Andromeda,
Beside the bears—Ursa Major, Ursa Minor—Capricorn, too,
Orion, with his belt so clear, and Aquarius, as well;
Can't find these constellations? Look for a clue!

Standing at the window, at one of Alberta's country farms,
Looking out serenely into the very dark, dark night,
We just marveled at what we miss living in the city,
Under the bright, bright glow of a very shiny streetlight!

The Onion

I peeled an onion today—to bake with the roast,
The left-over onion—my husband had with toast!

This fresh onion was quite large, just a nice workable size,
I started to take off the peel—tears came out of my eyes!

The faster I cut, the stronger the onion's smell filled the room,
By the time I was done, my eyes looked like they were in bloom!

Chopped in pieces, assembled around the roast in the pan,
The onion was now ready, and on went the overhead fan!

The smell—oh, how it lingered in the kitchen all day long,
But what a delicious addition to the roast—can't go wrong.

As I thought of this onion with its stinging smell so bold,
One that makes your eyes weep—thought of growing old.

As we walk through life's journey, some experiences sting,
Like the onion to our eyes—but these stings often bring ...

Wonderful experiences—like the roast's delicious smell,
That, through all our life, help us cope so very well.

Experiences that sting and linger in our personal life time,
I'm glad of my onion-weepy events—they were just fine!

Lynda Horvath

How Important is a Phone Call

The home phone does not ring as much any more,
Since we have cell phones and email and text,
But when it does surprise us both and loudly ring,
We often wonder—what possibly will be next?

Oh, it's a weird number on the call display,
Not a number we are at all familiar with,
Let's just let it ring and ring some more,
It must be some hilariously funny myth!

So, you answer one of these weird numbers
And find out that your computer is very sick,
It's got three viruses, it's ready to crater,
You respond with one quick, short click!

Then there's the companies with great treats,
Holidays, specials, contests—you're a winner!
Wouldn't be so bad to win something nice,
But the calls always seem to come during dinner!

And finally, the calls that you like—the special ones
From family and friends, their known numbers you see,
You delight in these calls, they excite you big time,
You're glad you have a phone—a 'connection' key!

Shoveling Snow!

Shoveling snow can be fun,
When one watches it
From inside their house.
It can be just a skiff,
Or it can be two feet deep,
It doesn't really matter
Because, regardless,
Two lovely young fellows
Will soon be here
With their big blowers
To get rid of it!
Usually, we would be
Out there as soon as
The last flake fell,
Blowing and shoveling,
Sweeping and chipping,
Till the sidewalk was as clean
As the kitchen floor!
This year, it would have been
All left up to me to
Keep the snow cleared

Lynda Horvath

On our walks and the neighbors, too,

Because my hubby's arm

Is laid up in a sling.

And, lo and behold,

We 'fixed' this dilemma—

This snow-shoveling thing!

After every snowfall,

Before you can turn around,

The walks are all clear

By our 'snow-shoveling' fellows,

And I am smiling!

A Hurried Life/A Retired Life

A hurried life is what we knew for sixty years,
Busy with home life, busier with life at work,
Up early, get home-life ready for the day,
And off to your job, often without a perk!

What kept us going, those eighteen hours,
Each and every day, without even a break?
I think it was knowing, that down the road,
A nice long break we would be able to take.

Amid lots of opportunities and experiences
To grow in this world, during these busy days,
We still had time to make some new friends,
And enjoy each other's unique, interesting ways.

Then, after watching the clock for so many years,
The time was coming to start to slow down a bit,
Getting ready for a new and different busy life,
Wondering how, together, hopefully, it just might fit.

Lynda Horvath

And then it came, the last day of our working career,
This busy-ness was about to be over, to be done,
We'll take a few weeks or months to change pace,
And learn how to have a little bit of any-time fun.

It didn't take long, this transition of our new life,
The visits, the trips to the country, coffee dates,
The walks, sitting to read a book or do a puzzle,
Such a vast difference—everything just waits!

Time is the difference-maker in this, our new life,
We can take as long as we want, whenever we want,
To do exactly what we want, as we want—such a treat,
Retirement, yes, it is so wonderful, let's go for a jaunt!

Just Keep Going

Sometimes you see people once a year,
Pick up the pieces of life to share,
Just keep going where you left off,
Fill your time together with care.

Recalling other friends we've met
In our journey together up to this day,
Laughing, crying, smiles and tears,
Each have added to our life's 'way'.

Over the years, we each have welcomed
New friends into our journey's road,
We've said 'good-bye' to other folk
Who have had to lighten life's load.

Sometimes these folk are your greatest
Life's encouragers, they can understand
That walking this earth is not easy
But it is great from-afar hand-in-hand.

We are thankful for our friends like these
Who come together with us, as we all can,
It's times like these that mean so much
Making memories over life's short span.

Lynda Horvath

Smoke!

We woke up this August morning,
And what did we first see—
A blanket of smoke over the city,
And this blanket covered even me!

The smoke is from the great fires,
From California and from B.C., too,
The smell just takes your breath away,
Many people are affected, not a few!

The sun is a bright orangey-red color,
But it has kept the temperatures down,
It's thirty above, but it doesn't feel that,
As a red hue just covers this big town!

There is no end in sight here at our place,
The fires just keep burning on and on,
We feel for the people directly affected,
Hopefully, these big fires are soon gone!

Another phenomenon of nature's plight,
One we can only accept and embrace,
This smoke is a pain, there's no doubt,
Soon it will be over, we'll accept it with grace.

Paths

Which path in life have you taken?
Or, have you taken many-a different one?
When a fork appeared in your 'life' road,
Were you able to carry on, having fun?

The definition of a 'path' is a narrow way,
That you can walk, run, hop or crawl,
And all paths are shaped by many people
Who venture through them, one and all.

Although one can go around a path,
Beside a path, or journey right in it,
The only way to enjoy a path, and to learn,
Is to face each path head-on, bit by bit.

Lynda Horvath

I have learned from a variety of paths in life,
The path of a young girl moving to a city,
Another of falling in love and marrying,
Then a 'single-mother of two' path, not pretty.

An education path to university and beyond,
A thirty-five year path in a classroom or two,
Forty-two years ago, a path that met a new love,
And, in all those years, we stumbled through.

The latest path is one of retirement, such fun,
And crossing paths with so many new folk,
Has made life so very worthwhile each day,
My life-paths—they have been awesome, no joke!

Ready to Give UP?

I woke up this morning,
Feeling my new, old age!
My hip and knee were sore,
Like I'd been in a cage!

Then my ankle, too,
With shooting pain,
My whole left side hurt,
Another day of this—again?

I tried to get out of bed,
What a chore that was!
Finally, feet moving ahead,
My head in a bit of fuzz!

Those kinks in my left side,
What a great pain they are,
But at least I am walking,
But maybe, today, not very far!

Lynda Horvath

Give me about an hour or so,
Maybe these kinks will go away;
I really don't want a full day of this,
If they should decide to stay!

The choices are very clear to me,
One can just 'put up' and be quiet;
Or lay down and forget the day,
Which, for me, just doesn't fit!

Pull up your chin and smile,
Get up and get at it, I say,
Oh, my, I'm sure very thankful
I don't have many days like today!

My Time is Valuable

What I do with my time these days is important,
Because I cannot get back a day or an hour;
Time passes so quickly, in the blink of an eye,
Before you know it, the milk has turned sour!

When one is at work, time seems to drag,
And one can't wait to do nothing, to retire;
At that time, it looks like a very swell gift,
To read a book, and watch the crackling fire.

However, now that I've spent ten years retired,
I realize more clearly how time is a treat;
One can do whatever, whenever, however,
Without even putting, out of bed, your feet.

That would do for a short while, I'd think,
It's more fun to get up, get out, get with it;
Life marches on, if you want it to or not,
So the best way to challenge it—don't sit!

There is so much to do, great things all about,
To keep your mind very active, your body, too;
Enjoying every minute, regardless of weather,
Every second counts, whatever you want to do!

Lynda Horvath

Worries

It's fun to look at your life and see
The unfinished parts that glare,
Those that still need some work,
Those that cry out—still there!

My biggest unfinished part is
A nice body, slender and slim,
Maybe a size 8 would do,
But that will always be a whim!

The next big hurdle is water,
Drinking it every day, and lots,
Would keep me 'moving' daily
And take away the stress-spots!

Yet another is buying clothes
That might enhance old me,
I cannot stand stores and the lack
Of clothes that might fit to a T!

One more, I worry about everyone,
If they are happy, content or glad,
I care that they are not hurting,
Regardless of me being sad!

So why do I worry, I have no clue,
I just know that it is a part of me,
Always has, always will be, I think,
I need to go on a worry-free spree!

Un-Comfy Chairs

We are spoiled—we love our chairs at home,
They recline, they are comfy, they are our fav's,
In our family room, the most-used in our house,
It is like they are in our man-and-woman caves!

Those comfy chairs can be reclined to many levels,
One can sit upright, or sit very relaxed and at rest,
Or one can have a snooze for an hour or two,
Whatever the need—they really are the very best!

In our winter abode, our chairs are just not as great,
They're not comfy, they're hard to relax on—no fun,
But our choices are minimal as to what is available,
And, these chairs are certainly better than none!

One learns to make the most of a situation, any one,
The option is to just complain—doesn't do any good,
Or learn to adjust—to your expectations of your life,
The last option is the best—keep positive, we should!

Yes, we will enjoy our comfy chairs when we return home,
That, for absolutely certain, is a very well-known fact,
We are spoiled, we know it well, we readily admit it,
But enjoying a simple life is our retirement pact!

Lynda Horvath

W's—Five of Them!

The five W's have always intrigued me—
They rule our life, or so it would seem!
They are important, there is no doubt,
For without them, we would not gleam!

First there is the **WHO** that is you and me,
We are the ones who we've decided to be;
The **WHO** in our lives, that's who we are,
And nothing can change us, near or far!

Then there is the **WHAT**, that makes us tick,
It's our inner being, our thoughts and love,
It's the **WHAT** that people often see in us,
Hopefully, fitting like a hand in a glove.

Next is the **WHEN** part of our short life,
Do we speak **WHEN** necessary, or not,
Do we help others **WHEN** they need it,
Are we 'there' only when we are caught?

And then there is the **WHERE** part of life,
It is our place of residence, our abode,
WHERE we can make a real difference,
If **WHERE** is a part of our life's-road.

And lastly, there is the **WHY** we are here,
Making some amazing choices—good ones,
That will make a fulfilling and beautiful life,
So we can count our blessings, by the tons!

Yesterday, Today, Tomorrow

Yesterday is just a memory
Of things we did that day—
The relaxing times of reading,
Visiting friends across the way,
Pulling weeds out in the garden,
Cleaning the house, if I may,
Cooking some creative meals,
Yesterday was great, it was OK!

Today is here, and what will I do—
Something that will be a gain,
Maybe washing some windows,
Oh! Can't because it's gonna rain!
Maybe making some cinnamon buns
For our neighbors—that's no pain!
Or, spending the day reading and writing,
That time spent would not be in vain!

Lynda Horvath

Now, tomorrow—it hasn't happened yet,
What will be the events, I don't have a clue,
Just know we are off to church in the morn,
We'll get there at ten bells, right on cue!
Then, maybe for lunch, we might decide
To find a restaurant that, to us, is new,
Visit with some friends, we might choose,
To have over in the aft or eve, not sure who!

So, there is yesterday, today, and tomorrow,
Our lives all in a concise, organized nutshell,
One is on crutches, the other has a sore leg,
But we are going to pretend we are very well,
Because what we're really doing is living
Our life, these days, as near as we can tell—
Each day we live is a treasure, a present,
So, let's celebrate and ring a big, loud bell!

COVID-19

It's been four weeks since we had
A dear friend enter our door;
And so we do ask each other,
"Are we prepared for much more!"

We love being with our friends,
We love sharing a coffee or meal;
We love seeing people very often;
It's friends who make our life real!

It's the physical contact we are missing,
As we partake in our social distance;
We would love to be able to give a hug,
Or even to high-five, and maybe dance!

So, thanks to FaceTime, email and text,
We can keep in contact with phone, too,
Just to hear voices, read special words,
Makes each day feel like it's so new!

We will make the best of it, we always do,
We will hunker down and do our very best,
To help our world, country and province,
To put this horrible virus to a definite rest!

Lynda Horvath

Missing Friends

We are missing our friends these days,
On a variety of special 'friendly' ways!

We do miss having people in for a meal,
Sad and lonely, today, is how we feel!

There's the neighbors, in for coffee,
Who we regularly like to visit and see.

Then there's our friends from church,
We all feel like we're each on a perch!

Missing the weekly contact, and more,
Missing them coming through our door!

Our dear 'old' school friends and chums,
No coffee, visits, buffets—just ho-hums!

And then there's folks we often see,
We've known for many years—from A to Zee!

Even an hour or two, to see their dear face,
Would help fill our very long, daily, space!

One never realizes how precious friends are,
Until you can't see them—not even from afar!

When we DO get together again, not sure when,
It will be a beautiful time—again and again!!

It Continues!

As the days of 2020 roll by,
Sometimes so very, very slow,
We make the most of our time,
Doing the best we absolutely know!

COVID-19—nothing's at all new—
Stay home, stay inside, stay safe,
Keep happy, keep busy, keep calm,
Eat lots? Nobody's looking like a waif!

The situation in the world is so grim,
The numbers of deaths and cases,
Just keep growing higher and higher,
Sad, sad looks on many, many faces!

Such confusion, such grim reminders,
People cannot seem to agree on what
Is important, or timely, or even very real—
Part of the world is in a deep rut!

Lynda Horvath

I'm so thankful we live where we do,
With leaders who are trying their best,
To keep us safe and secure, at home,
To give us some peace and some rest.

If we all pull together through this virus,
And not apart as we see just to our south,
We will manage this 'new normal' just fine,
With positive words right from our mouth!

We have all learned a lot during this time,
Of how to reach out by email and text,
Of how to spend time wisely, at home,
Oh how, with friends and family, to connect!

.

Feelings

I'm trying to write a little poem
To explain my feelings these days;
I'm having a hard time thinking how
Life has changed—in so many ways.

The biggest change, the one not nice,
Is that we can't see any dear friend;
We talk, chat and email, but never see
Each other—will this 'change' never end?

We go for groceries only every two weeks,
We go early, carefully managing to stay,
In the aisles allotted, getting our needs,
Before we get to the shielded place to pay.

Not everyone is taking this seriously,
But we would rather be safe, than bend
The rules that have been given us
To help get the world on the mend!

Thank goodness, spring has now arrived,
And we can enjoy the sun's bright rays;
Working and digging outside in the yard,
Listening to the chirps of the bluejays!

Lots of little jobs have finally been done,
As right at home, we did—24/7—spend;
Over this last month of social-distancing,
Our 'new normal' feelings have no end!

Lynda Horvath

Watching the News!

IF you want to get confused,
Just watch the news on TV;
There is a great wide variety
Of differing opinions to see!

Some say to lock down,
Stay at home by yourselves;
Other say to just carry on,
Don't become little elves!

Others say to wear a mask
When you go out to a store;
Others—that is unnecessary;
Why do you do anything more?

Well, our health officials say
To keep healthy and safe,
Obey the rules they've given,
So we don't become a waif!

We've spent over a month
Seeing no one at all—no one;
That is the hardest part of life,
Hopefully, this soon will be done!

So, we'll just keep watching the news,
Sorting the 'garbage' and the true,
We'll listen carefully to the experts,
Amid all this, we WILL come through!

Statistics

It has been two months—long and lonely,
Since this COVID-19 hit our land;
The tragedies in the world are huge,
Growing every day, like sifting sand!

Three million folks have it world-wide,
Over one million in the U. S. of A.;
Canada, just over fifty thousand;
All these high numbers are not OK!

Even our Alberta, five thousand folk,
Have been diagnosed, to this date;
Just hope these numbers will stop;
No more rising—please, shut the gate!

Lynda Horvath

The numbers seem to be slowing down,
A little bit more each very-long week;
But we can't ever get too complacent,
The numbers could once-again peak!

Watching the numbers this last month,
Has been interesting, to say the least;
People all over the world are trying
To control this very-ugly 'virus-beast'!

We are hoping and praying that no one,
No one we know within our friend-base,
Will become a 'virus-statistic' this year,
But can stay safe in their own space!

Sitting Outside

I am sitting outside right now,
Enjoying the sun and the breeze,
The fountain is gurgling water,
And I feel like I could sneeze!

The sparrows are chirping away,
They talk to their babies, we think,
They're flying around the birdhouses,
In and out they fly, quick as a wink!

They seem to be talking to each other,
They just constantly chirp and speak,
I wish I knew what they were saying,
As they flap their wings and their beak.

It is so quiet out here this morning,
Very few cars, no traffic sounds at all,
This COVID-19 has made a huge change,
In the noise level around us—now very small!

Lynda Horvath

We do see more people walking outside,
Than we ever had previously before,
Because they are stuck at home,
It's probably nice to get out their door.

I am so glad spring has finally arrived,
And we are not stuck inside our home,
We can't go anywhere, but enjoy our yard,
It is a very relaxing bird-and-plant dome.

So, we make the most of every precious day,
Whether the sun shines or whether it rains,
For each twenty-four hours, enjoy your space,
Forget the COVID, and your arthritis pains!

Today is Sunday, May 17, 2020

Today is Sunday, May 17, 20-20,
And life is so different and new,
Sometimes we think to ourselves,
Now, today, what shall we do?

We can't think of going to church,
Where, with our friends, we do gather,
We sure do miss seeing them,
Worshipping together, we would rather!

And then, often, we would go out for lunch,
With a couple so dear and special to us,
We share laughter, some tears, always fun,
Together, for an hour or so, no fuss!

And then, in the afternoon, often a visit,
With friends, some from far away,
We then gather together for a meal,
Usually at five, at our favorite buffet!

Well, the church gatherings are over,
Possibly for quite a lengthy time;
The after-church lunches are gone,
And the buffet, too—saving a dime!

Lynda Horvath

So, church we can watch it on-line,
We get great messages and worship,
From our church, and three others,
Just on the TV, need to channel-flip!

The one thing that never changes—yeah!
Is, around supper-time, the phone does ring,
Each Sunday we chat with family in Vancouver,
And that makes our hearts truly sing!

Our times together with our friends,
Will be even more special and fun,
When we can all get-together one day,
And chat, laugh, and sit in the sun!

This day really is great to just think
Of the privileges we have at hand,
Make the most of each day—yes, today,
And realize—ain't life really quite grand!

We're in a Valley

We are in a huge valley right now,
One like we have never seen before;
We seemed to get there pretty quickly,
Before we could even shut the door!

Now, I do know a little about valleys,
They're between two mountains or hills,
The trip from the valley to the hill-top
Is hard, takes a lot of determined wills!

The sides are often almost straight-up,
The climb is grueling, hard and tough,
But, so rewarding when we reach the top,
Even if we have to sit, and huff and puff.

When one looks down from the top
And can see how far you have come,
The journey was definitely worth it,
Hard work always pays—don't be glum!

The good top soil on the top of a hill,
During snow, sleet, storms and rain,
Slides down to the valley, making it rich,
And fertile, always to our great gain.

So, we are in the middle of COVID,
And social justice, valleys right now,
Not one, but now even two, is upon us,
How do we deal with these two—how?

Lynda Horvath

Every week is different in this valley,
We learn something new each day;
We listen, we hear, we make decisions,
To help us choose a 'new normal' way!

The one thing we know for certain today,
Is that in this valley we will have grown,
We will have learned how to cope anew,
How, individually, what we can condone.

One day, we will get back to that hill-top,
Remember the valley experiences we had,
The ones that were new, were unsettling,
But we can now say, they weren't so bad!

Mosaics

Mosaics are made from broken pieces,
But they are still a work of art;
Each piece means something special,
From someone's very dearest heart!

Each piece has a very special story,
Each has a story of its very own;
Some stories we may have heard,
Some stories will never be known!

Each tiny piece in a beautiful mosaic,
Is of its very own special color or hue;
When these are all put together as one,
A beautiful picture comes through!

Where do these tiny pieces come from?
They come from a variety of places,
All put together to make something nice,
Each piece will fill in all the mosaic spaces!

Mosaics take hours to make, to piece together,
But every second and minute is so worthwhile;
'Cuz countless people, regardless of the scene,
Will appreciate the beautifully, intricate mosaic-style!

Lynda Horvath

This World ...

Today my heart is horribly breaking
For our dear, dear planet--our world!
It seems so much 'stuff' is happening,
So very, very much is coming unfurled!

We started the year 20-20 quite OK,
Things were rolling along quite fine;
Then Coronavirus, COVID-19, hit us,
Giving us all a horrible and sad sign.

People soon became sick, very sick,
People soon started dying, not a few;
So, we all became much more careful
Trying to watch everything we would do!

We stayed home as much as we could,
Only going for groceries every ten days;
Going early in the morning, senior time,
Trying to change our age-old ways!

Then the masks—our exciting new attire,
To keep everyone safe, as much as we can;
Keeping those germs away from each other,
Trying to help keep safe, our fellow-man.

People off work, many losing their jobs,
Families now stuck at home all together,
Schools totally closed, parents now teachers,
Sometimes life becomes a bit of a GRRRRRR!

... more

Many businesses closed all of their doors,
And many will never be able to open again;
So many people laid-off, no money for them,
This devastating virus—causing so much pain.

Then the social justice issues in this world,
Have been devastatingly horrible to see,
Watching people get hurt, shot and abused,
So much of it because of someone's knee!

Bad choices by many, especially from the top,
Caused protests—some peaceful, some not,
Caused decisions that were totally off-hand,
Caused destruction and devastation—a lot!

Many angry people, fighting for their rights,
All across the world, from both far and near;
Making the news every night, sad but true,
Causing a whole lot of outrageous fear.

Now into week sixteen, since the virus hit,
The numbers of deaths and cases are rising;
Many are not taking this virus seriously,
And we have a long way to go—no compromising!

Will we ever be done this self-isolation, masks,
Social-distancing, staying home, no friends?
Our 'new normal' these days is hard to accept,
We just hope this Coronavirus scare soon ends!

And now, another blow as we listen to the news,
Two countries at odds—soldiers' lives at great harm,
I just can't believe what is happening out there,
It frightens me to the core—causing much alarm!

Lynda Horvath

Countries in conflict—will it never ever end?
There is always something they are at war about,
Always someone ticked-off mad at someone else,
Do either one of the leaders have any sensible clout?

So, today, this world is in quite a visible mess,
And we are not sure how long it might last;
Our job, it seems, is to keep healthy and safe,
Until this Coronavirus—COVID-19–is long past!

Index of Poems

About me

From the time I was a young girl on an Alberta farm, I wanted to be a teacher! Luckily, my dream came true, and I was privileged to spend thirty-five wonderful years in elementary classrooms. Writing, and especially poetry, was a favourite part of working with creative minds.

When I was fortunate enough to retire, writing became even more important to me. So, as a challenge to myself, I decided to take a 'slice of my life' each day and create a poem. The journey became more and more exciting, and soon I had over five hundred poems–ranging from ideas such as 'the birds in the back of the yard' or 'the supper dilemma' or even 'the weather'!

My friends tell me that I can write a poem about anything and everything–give me a topic, and the creative juices start to flow! Family and friends have encouraged me to share my life experiences and 'reflections' in a book, so that became my next challenge!

As I share my life, through these poems, you no doubt will be able to relate to many of my experiences in your own life! Enjoy!

To order more copies of this book, find books by other
Canadian authors, or make inquiries about publishing your
own book, contact PageMaster at:

PageMaster Publication Services Inc.
11340-120 Street, Edmonton, AB T5G 0W5
books@pagemaster.ca
780-425-9303

catalogue and e-commerce store
PageMasterPublishing.ca/Shop